CALIFORNIA
TRIVIA

CALIFORNIA TRIVIA

COMPILED BY LUCY POSHEK AND ROGER NAYLOR

Rutledge Hill Press®
Nashville, Tennessee

Published by Rutledge Hill Press, a Division of Thomas Nelson Inc., P.O.Box 141000, Nashville, Tennessee 37214.
Distributed in Canada by H. B. Fenn & Company, Ltd., 34 Nixon Road, Bolton, Ontario L7E 1W2.

Typography by Compass Communications, Inc., Nashville, Tennessee.

Library of Congress Cataloging-in-Publication Data

Poshek, Lucy.
   California trivia / compiled by Lucy Poshek and Roger
Naylor.
      p.   cm.
   ISBN 1-55853-679-5 (pbk.)
     1. California—Miscellanea.   I. Naylor, Roger, 1933–   .
  II. Title.
  F861.5.P67   1998
  979.4—dc21   98-39434
                                      CIP

Printed in the United States of America
1 2 3 4 5 - 08 07 06 05 04

PREFACE

Can you think of any other state that rivals California in its geographic diversity, historical color, and entertainment status? The Golden State is a veritable treasure chest of fascinating details, which made *California Trivia* a pleasure for us to compile and write. We think that even California natives will be surprised by some of the tidbits found in this book. As long-time residents of this state, we considered ourselves pretty knowledgeable on the subject, but we were amazed to discover the wealth of cultural, scientific, and athletic contributions California has made to the world.

For their contributions, feedback, and support, we wish to acknowledge our thanks to Jeanne and Buffy Naylor, John Porter, Ruth Hanks, Linda Lampson, and the Meierding family—the ultimate trivia buffs—especially Mark, Bill, Nina, Emily, Julie, and David.

We hope you enjoy reading *California Trivia* as much as we did putting it together.

—Lucy Poshek and Roger Naylor

TABLE OF CONTENTS

CALIFORNIA
TRIVIA

GEOGRAPHY

C H A P T E R   O N E

Q. Which city lies farther east—Reno or Los Angeles?

A. Los Angeles.

Q. When and how was the Salton Sea, California's largest lake, created?

A. In 1905, when the Colorado River flooded.

Q. How did Tarzana get its name?

A. Edgar Rice Burroughs, who wrote the Tarzan stories, founded the town.

Q. The Sacramento River and what other major river join near the capital city?

A. San Joaquin.

Q. Anaheim was settled by immigrants from where?

A. Rhineland. The city's name is German for "home by the river."

Q. How high is Mount Whitney, the highest point in the contiguous United States?

A. 14,495 feet.

Q. Where is the lowest elevation in the Western Hemisphere?

A. Near Badwater, in Death Valley, at 282 feet below sea level.

Q. California's highest and lowest points are how far apart?

A. Less than one hundred miles.

Q. How many different kinds of fruits and vegetables are grown by California farmers?

A. Approximately two hundred.

Q. In 1826, Native Americans comprised 98 percent of the territory's population. What percentage of California's current population is Native American?

A. Less than 1 percent.

Q. In terms of area, what is the largest county in the state?

A. San Bernardino.

Q. What is known as "the crookedest street in the world"?

A. Lombard Street, in San Francisco.

Q. What percentage of California's population live in rural areas?

A. Nine percent.

Q. California trails Oregon and what other state in forest products?

A. Washington.

Q. How much of the U.S. wine production comes from California wineries?

A. About 90 percent.

Q. California's coastline, from Oregon to Mexico, measures how many miles?

A. About 840.

Q. The publication of the first detailed, accurate map of the American West was prompted by what historic event?

A. The California Gold Rush.

Q. What local resource did the Yurok tribe use to build their homes in Northern California?

A. Redwood.

Q. Where do the San Joaquin and Sacramento Rivers merge?

A. Suisun Bay.

Q. Where does California rank nationally in terms of air pollution?

A. The worst.

———— ⚭ ————

Q. What is another name for the Orange County Airport?

A. The John Wayne Airport.

———— ⚭ ————

Q. How many U.S. states border California?

A. Three—Oregon, Nevada, and Arizona.

———— ⚭ ————

Q. What was the highest recorded temperature in the state, registered in Death Valley in 1913?

A. 134 degrees Fahrenheit.

———— ⚭ ————

Q. On what type of landform is the town of Coronado situated?

A. A peninsula.

———— ⚭ ————

Q. In terms of area, what is the smallest county in the state?

A. San Francisco.

———— ⚭ ————

Q. What percentage of lumber does California provide for the nation?

A. About 10 percent.

Q. Which University of California campus is the smallest geographically?

A. UCLA.

Q. What California county forms a perfect rectangle?

A. Modoc.

Q. What is the northernmost and last mission founded in the state?

A. San Francisco Solano Mission, in Sonoma.

Q. What poetic phrase did Jack London give to Sonoma?

A. Valley of the Moon.

Q. What are the two major mountain ranges of California?

A. The Cascade Mountains and the Sierra Nevada.

Q. What is the popular interpretation of how the city of Azusa got its name?

A. It has "everything from A to Z in the USA."

Q. What was the nickname of the Santa Clara Valley before it became known as Silicon Valley?

A. The Valley of Heavenly Delights.

Q. What are the highest sand dunes in California?

A. Eureka Sand Dunes (seven hundred feet high) in Death Valley National Park.

———⊗∞———

Q. What is the second-highest mountain in the state?

A. Mount Williamson, at 14,375 feet.

———⊗∞———

Q. California has how many counties?

A. Fifty-eight.

———⊗∞———

Q. How many state forests are in California?

A. Eight.

———⊗∞———

Q. What two large California lakes extend into other states?

A. Tahoe (shared with Nevada) and Goose (shared with Oregon).

———⊗∞———

Q. What is the northernmost latitude of California?

A. Forty-two degrees.

———⊗∞———

Q. In what U.S. state is there a town named California?

A. Pennsylvania.

Q. Which Southern California town features an oil museum?

A. Santa Paula.

⸺∞⸺

Q. What county is the nation's largest manufacturing center?

A. Los Angeles.

⸺∞⸺

Q. What was the nation's first state park?

A. Yosemite, established in 1864. (It became a national park in 1890.)

⸺∞⸺

Q. Of the forty highest waterfalls in the world, how many are in Yosemite National Park?

A. Nine.

⸺∞⸺

Q. Found in California, what is one of the world's oldest lakes?

A. Mono, seven hundred thousand years old.

⸺∞⸺

Q. In addition to the Mojave, what is California's other large desert?

A. The Colorado Desert.

⸺∞⸺

Q. What street address would you give a cab driver to go to Disneyland?

A. 1313 Harbor Boulevard, Anaheim.

Q. Which Native-American tribe lived in the Mojave Desert for thousands of years?

A. Fort Mojave.

———— ∞∞ ————

Q. Where is the westernmost terminus for the Central Pacific Railroad?

A. Oakland.

———— ∞∞ ————

Q. What city is considered the world capital of agricultural business, generating $3 billion per year?

A. Fresno.

———— ∞∞ ————

Q. On what river did the Yurok tribe rely for salmon fishing?

A. Klamath.

———— ∞∞ ————

Q. The two main farming regions of California are the Central Valley and what other valley?

A. Imperial.

———— ∞∞ ————

Q. What is the location of the controversial dam that the city of San Francisco voted to build in the early 1900s?

A. The Hetch Hetchy Valley, in Yosemite.

———— ∞∞ ————

Q. What black volcanic glass was found in the mountains of Mono County, used by Indians for arrow points?

A. Obsidian.

Q. When was the Pacific Standard Time zone established?

A. In 1869.

Q. What was the main source of water for the Mojave Indians?

A. The Colorado River.

Q. From what is one-fifth of California's electricity generated?

A. Water power.

Q. What California irrigation system is the largest in the world?

A. The Central Valley Project, linking more than thirteen hundred reservoirs.

Q. How is water carried from the Northern California mountains to Southern California?

A. Via the California Aqueduct.

Q. What is the "Okie capital" of California?

A. Bakersfield.

Q. What San Francisco army base is now a national park and historic landmark?

A. The Presidio.

Q. What city has the largest Spanish-speaking population north of Mexico City?

A. Los Angeles.

Q. Which resort offers the only naturally carbonated warm mineral springs in North America?

A. Vichy Hot Springs Resort, near Ukiah.

Q. What Northern California town was built on seven steep hills?

A. Nevada City.

Q. Which country outside of the United States relies most heavily on California's agriculture, generating $6 billion per year?

A. Japan.

Q. Which U.S. Air Force base is located in the Mojave Desert?

A. Edwards.

Q. Which direction does the current flow along the California coastline?

A. Southward.

Q. What is the only natural lake in Santa Barbara County?

A. Zaca.

Q. What East Coast state is parallel with San Francisco in latitude?

A. Virginia.

Q. How far is Catalina Island from the mainland at its closest point?

A. Nineteen miles.

Q. How many peaks in the Sierra Nevada are more than fourteen thousand feet high?

A. Fourteen.

Q. What sets the Tehachapi Mountains apart from most California ranges?

A. Referred to as a transverse range, they run east and west.

Q. What unusual rock outcroppings northeast of Newhall have served as a backdrop for many movies, including *The Flintstones*?

A. Vasquez Rocks.

Q. What California island is derived from the Spanish phrase for "the Island of the Pelicans"?

A. Alcatraz *(La Isla de los Alcatraces)*.

Q. What percentage of California land is covered by forests?

A. About 40 percent.

Q. If California were a nation, where would it rank in total economic production?

A. Tenth-highest in the world.

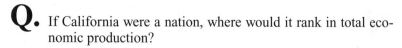

Q. At which winery were European varietal grapes first grown in America?

A. Buena Vista, near Sonoma.

Q. What Southern California city's name is derived from the Spanish word for "good fortune"?

A. Ventura *(San Buenaventura)*.

Q. Lined with restaurants such as Chez Panisse, what street in Berkeley is known as the birthplace of California cuisine?

A. Shattuck Avenue.

Q. What three crops beginning with "A" are grown almost exclusively in California?

A. Artichokes, almonds, and apricots.

Q. As the crow flies, what is the greatest north-south distance in California?

A. 646 miles.

Q. Who named the strait spanned by the famous bridge, the Golden Gate?

A. Gen. John C. Frémont, after the Golden Horn of Istanbul.

Q. Which two California valleys grow all of the nation's dates?

A. Imperial and Coachella.

Q. In terms of area, where does California rank in the nation?

A. Third, at 158,869 square miles.

Q. What state beach lies just south of Nipomo Dunes, where the sand dunes reach as high as five hundred feet?

A. Point LaSalle.

Q. What was the original name of America's first freeway?

A. The Arroyo Seco Parkway (now the Pasadena Freeway), built in 1940.

Q. What area of California produces more than half of the flower seeds sold in the world?

A. Lompoc Valley.

Q. What is the largest beach in Marin County?

A. Stinson.

Q. The Channel Islands National Park is comprised of what five islands?

A. San Miguel, Santa Rosa, Santa Cruz, Anacapa, and Santa Barbara.

Q. How did Calistoga get its name?

A. San Francisco newspaper tycoon Sam Brannan combined "California" with "Saratoga" when he built a spa there in 1859.

Q. Which Native-American tribe lived along the Sacramento River two hundred years ago and still exists in Tuolumne today?

A. Miwok.

Q. What is the state's most valuable crop, adding about $600 million a year to the economy?

A. Tomatoes.

Q. The average annual rainfall in California varies how much from southern desert to northern coast?

A. From less than two inches in the deserts to 140 inches along the northern coast.

Q. What Northern California state park is famous for its beach of smooth agate, jasper, and jade rocks?

A. Patrick's Point.

Q. What is the highest highway pass in California?

A. Tioga, at 9,945 feet.

Q. What town has the largest lumber mill in the United States?

A. Scotia.

Q. What is the name of the Amtrak train that connects Los Angeles to the Bay Area?

A. The Coast Starlight.

Q. Where does California rank nationally in its production of oranges?

A. Second, behind Florida.

Q. Where did California's first navel oranges come from?

A. Brazil.

Q. What percentage of Southern California suburbanites travel more than one hour to get to work?

A. Seven percent.

Q. San Mateo and Santa Cruz Counties produce 90 percent of what crop in the nation?

A. Brussels sprouts.

Q. What unique mode of transportation was used throughout the new Southern California community that Abbott Kinney established in 1904?

A. Gondolas, in Venice.

Q. What is the third-largest lake in California?

A. Clair Engle, in Shasta-Trinity National Forest.

Q. Where is the second-smallest cathedral in the world?

A. Laguna Beach.

———∞∞∞———

Q. Where is the shortest ferry ride in the state?

A. The Balboa Island to Balboa Peninsula ferry (about two minutes).

———∞∞∞———

Q. What is the largest island in San Francisco Bay?

A. Angel.

———∞∞∞———

Q. Of the nation's twenty most populous cities, how many are in California?

A. Four—Los Angeles, San Diego, San Jose, and San Francisco.

———∞∞∞———

Q. The Central Valley's agricultural success is aided by what kind of soil?

A. Alluvial.

———∞∞∞———

Q. What is California's leading field crop?

A. Cotton.

———∞∞∞———

Q. Of every ten Asian Americans in the United States, how many live in California?

A. Four.

Q. What's the name of the highway that begins at Mono Lake and ascends thirty-two hundred feet in twelve miles?

A. Lee Vining Canyon Highway.

―――∞∞∞―――

Q. Where does California's marijuana crop rank among the states?

A. First.

―――∞∞∞―――

Q. What percentage of the state's water comes from Northern California?

A. Seventy-five percent.

―――∞∞∞―――

Q. California produces what percentage of the wine and raisins in the nation?

A. More than 90 percent.

―――∞∞∞―――

Q. What town has the lowest elevation in the Western Hemisphere?

A. Calipatria, California (Route 115, north of El Centro), at 184 feet below sea level.

―――∞∞∞―――

Q. Middle Palisade Mountain in the Sierra Nevada is also known as what?

A. Disappointment Peak.

―――∞∞∞―――

Q. In the late nineteenth century, what city in California was nicknamed the "coffee capital of the world"?

A. San Francisco.

Q. California's first toll road was named what?

A. The Foothill Transportation Corridor, built in 1993 in Orange County.

———∽∾∾———

Q. Of foreign countries, which owns the most agricultural land in California?

A. The United Kingdom.

———∽∾∾———

Q. Although not native to California, what is the largest tribe of Native Americans living in the state today?

A. Cherokee.

———∽∾∾———

Q. What really goes on behind the faux high-rises and palm trees on the islands just offshore from Long Beach?

A. Oil drilling.

———∽∾∾———

Q. In terms of area, what is the second-largest county in California?

A. Inyo.

———∽∾∾———

Q. Which hotel boasts both the lowest elevation and the only borax museum in the world?

A. Furnace Creek Ranch, in Death Valley, at 178 feet below sea level.

———∽∾∾———

Q. What is California's mean (average) elevation?

A. Twenty-nine hundred feet.

Q. What is the largest reservoir in the State Water Project?

A. Lake Oroville.

———❧———

Q. What is the smallest and least-visited national park in California?

A. The Channel Islands.

———❧———

Q. What is the smallest national monument in California?

A. Cabrillo National Monument.

———❧———

Q. What is the only national seashore in California?

A. Point Reyes.

———❧———

Q. What is the largest town below sea level in the nation?

A. El Centro, at forty-five feet below sea level.

———❧———

Q. The combined San Francisco and San Pablo Bays have how many toll bridges?

A. Five.

———❧———

Q. In terms of dollars per mile, what was the most expensive road ever built?

A. The Century Freeway (or Glenn Anderson Freeway) in Los Angeles, built at $127 million per mile.

Q. In terms of attendance, what is the most popular state park in California?

A. Old Town San Diego State Historic Park.

Q. What little-known wilderness park was created in southeast California in 1994?

A. Algodones Dunes (also known as Imperial Sand Dunes).

Q. What mountain range runs along the southern Humboldt County coast?

A. King.

Q. The federal government owns what percentage of all California land?

A. Nearly 45 percent.

Q. Which Native-American reservation is the largest in California?

A. Hoopa Valley, in Humboldt County.

Q. What percentage of the state is classified as desert?

A. Twenty-four percent.

Q. In terms of population, what is the smallest county in California?

A. Sierra.

Q. What area has been nicknamed "the Salad Bowl of the Nation"?

A. The Salinas Valley.

Q. What is the cooperative of over six thousand citrus growers in Arizona and California called?

A. Sunkist.

Q. Which California state university campus is located on a former military base?

A. California State University at Monterey Bay (formerly Fort Ord).

Q. Near what California river lies one of the principal regions of the nation for growing Easter lillies?

A. Smith.

Q. What mountain east of Mount Baldy is named after the founder of the Boy Scouts?

A. Baden-Powell.

Q. In terms of latitude, Los Angeles is parallel with what African capital city?

A. Rabat, Morocco.

Q. What Southern California city is named for the Roman goddess of fruit?

A. Pomona.

Q. What Ventura County mountains are called by a name meaning "many gophers"?

A. Topatopa, above the Ojai Valley.

Q. What is the largest national park in the contiguous United States?

A. Death Valley.

Q. What Southern California town has the same name as a Canadian province?

A. Ontario.

Q. The fossil-laden Carrizo Badlands are situated in what state park?

A. Anza-Borrego Desert.

Q. On what livestock resource is Brawley's economy based?

A. Cattle.

Q. What town features the historic Swinging Bridge connecting the town's two sections?

A. Arroyo Grande.

Q. Coaling Station A, which began as a coal-loading point for the Southern Pacific Railroad Company, eventually grew into what town?

A. Coalinga.

Q. In what area of California are more turkeys raised than anywhere else in the country?

A. Fresno.

Q. What Gold Rush town has gone by the names of "Savage's Diggings" and "Garrotte"?

A. Groveland.

Q. Chaos Crags, Chaos Jumbles, and Bumpass Hell are situated in what national park?

A. Lassen.

Q. What is the name of the settlement at Catalina's isthmus?

A. Two Harbors.

Q. Named after the first judge of Los Angeles, what block-long street is one of the oldest in the city?

A. Olvera.

Q. What is America's tallest building west of Chicago?

A. The First Interstate World Center, in Los Angeles.

Q. The mountains situated in Mohave National Preserve are named after what state?

A. New York.

Q. What is the easternmost point of California?

A. Parker Dam.

Q. What is the world's shortest railway?

A. Angel's Flight Railway, a one-minute ride in Los Angeles.

Q. What scenic river runs through the Plumas National Forest?

A. Feather.

Q. What national forest is set between Kings Canyon and Yosemite National Parks?

A. Sierra.

Q. The profile of what triple-peaked mountain in Northern California is said to resemble a sleeping Native-American girl?

A. Tamalpais.

Q. What California town has the same name as the state motto?

A. Eureka.

Q. What "flavor" are the mountains east of the Salton Sea?

A. Chocolate (the Chocolate Mountains).

Q. San Francisco rests on how many hills?

A. Forty.

———— ∞ ————

Q. Stockton celebrates what vegetable in an annual festival?

A. Asparagus.

———— ∞ ————

Q. What new name did the city of El Toro adopt in 1991?

A. Lake Forest.

———— ∞ ————

Q. What is the nickname for Alcatraz Island?

A. The Rock.

———— ∞ ————

Q. With more than thirty million people, where does California's population rank nationally?

A. First.

———— ∞ ————

Q. In what city is the U.S. Navy's largest operational complex?

A. San Diego.

———— ∞ ————

Q. Considering the latitude, are the ocean waters along California generally warm or cold?

A. Cold, because the prevailing current brings the water south from Alaska.

Q. Castroville is known for what agricultural crop?

A. Artichokes.

———— ⊗ ————

Q. San Francisco, known for its showers, records what average annual rainfall?

A. Twenty-two inches.

———— ⊗ ————

Q. After those of Mexican descent, what is the second-most-common ancestry of California's population?

A. German.

———— ⊗ ————

Q. What is the highest unbroken waterfall in Yosemite National Park?

A. Ribbon Falls, at 1,612 feet.

———— ⊗ ————

Q. Despite all of California's "firsts," the title for total road mileage goes to which state?

A. Texas, with 305,690 miles to California's 164,300.

———— ⊗ ————

Q. What lighthouse sits at the northern end of the San Andreas fault?

A. Point Arena.

———— ⊗ ————

Q. What town was founded by the Danish-American Corporation in 1911?

A. Solvang.

Q. What is the remote stretch along the Humboldt-Mendocino coastline often called?

A. The Lost Coast.

Q. Which state produces substantially more gold than second-ranked California?

A. Nevada.

Q. By analyzing tree rings, scientists have determined that California's longest drought occurred when?

A. Between approximately 1250 and 1350.

Q. There are how many Native-American reservations in California?

A. 108.

Q. What military base has created the largest ground-contamination problem in the nation?

A. McClellan Air Force Base, in Sacramento.

Q. What mountains rise up from Big Sur?

A. Santa Lucia.

Q. What is the principal source of energy used in California?

A. Petroleum accounts for 50 percent, while natural gas trails at 30 percent.

Q. Where is the new California Spaceport, a commercial space-launch facility?

A. Vandenberg Air Force Base.

———∞———

Q. An original Spanish land grant in the eighteenth century reserved the right of access for every Los Angeles resident to what natural resource?

A. Tar, from the La Brea Tar Pits (used for roof and sail repairs).

———∞———

Q. Since Santa Clara County was "transformed" into Silicon Valley, what has been the effect on its per capita income?

A. Now the highest in California.

———∞———

Q. What changed the Southern California citrus industry to a year-round venture?

A. The introduction of Valencia oranges.

———∞———

Q. What Southern California town has long been especially known for growing avocados?

A. Fallbrook.

———∞———

Q. The nearly obsolescent term *Chinese gooseberry* referred to what California-grown fruit?

A. The kiwi.

———∞———

Q. With what did Luther Burbank begin his world-renowned business?

A. Ten potatoes, brought from the family farm in Massachusetts.

Q. What group of small islands is located about thirty miles west of San Francisco?

A. Farallon.

Q. What is the westernmost county in the state?

A. Humboldt.

Q. The name of what California town is Spanish for *butterfly*?

A. Mariposa.

Q. What is the name of SR198 as it enters Sequoia National Park?

A. Generals Highway.

ENTERTAINMENT

C H A P T E R   T W O

Q. An abandoned refrigerator car in Bakersfield was the birthplace of what country singer in 1937?

A. Merle Haggard.

Q. Of James Ellroy's novels about Los Angeles after dark, which one was made into an acclaimed movie?

A. *L. A. Confidential.*

Q. What three stops were called out by Mel Blanc as a train station announcer on *The Jack Benny Program*?

A. Anaheim, Azusa, and Cucamonga.

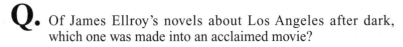

Q. What Santa Monica-born movie star later served as U.S. ambassador to Ghana and Czechoslovakia?

A. Shirley Temple Black.

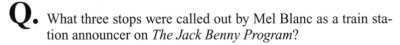

Q. Where did James Dean go to grammar school?

A. Brentwood Elementary School, in Los Angeles.

Q. Hollywood first gained a lead over Europe in the filmmaking industry because of what historic event?

A. World War I.

Q. What San Francisco museum is devoted to nostalgic television commercials?

A. The Museum of Modern Mythology.

Q. In a famous California folk song, whose father was "a miner, forty-niner"?

A. Clementine.

Q. What did Lawrence Welk's personalized California license plate say?

A. A1ANA2.

Q. In the 1936 movie *San Francisco*, who co-starred with Clark Gable and Spencer Tracy and belted out, "San Francisco, it's good to be home again"?

A. Jeanette MacDonald.

Q. Helendale has been the site of what entertaining annual event for more than forty years?

A. The Annual Burlesque Reunion.

Q. What half of a 1960s singing duo became mayor of Palm Springs and later a U.S. congressman?

A. Sonny Bono.

Q. What late-night talk show host used to set up a hidden camera at Hollywood and Vine during his show, then ad-lib about passersby?

A. Steve Allen.

Q. Francis Ford Coppola started what film studio in San Francisco in the late 1960s?

A. American Zoetrope.

Q. What California rock promoter shared the same name as a famous evangelist?

A. Bill Graham.

Q. The world championship crab races are held in what town every February?

A. Crescent City.

Q. After the bombing of Pearl Harbor, what sign did Jack Warner have painted on the roof of his hangar-like Burbank studio?

A. "Lockheed Thataway."

Q. What USC whiz kid won the third National Student Film Festival with his short, *THX: 4EB/Electronic Labyrinth*?

A. George Lucas.

Q. Where was *Same Time, Next Year* filmed?

A. The Heritage House in Little River, near Mendocino.

Q. What California rock group performed the 1966 hit "L. A. Woman"?

A. The Doors.

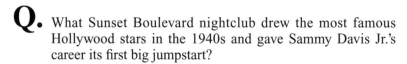

Q. What Sunset Boulevard nightclub drew the most famous Hollywood stars in the 1940s and gave Sammy Davis Jr.'s career its first big jumpstart?

A. Ciro's.

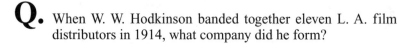

Q. When W. W. Hodkinson banded together eleven L. A. film distributors in 1914, what company did he form?

A. Paramount.

Q. In the film *Annie Hall*, when Woody Allen makes one of his few sojourns to California, he grows jealous of a mellow Hollywood character played by what songwriter?

A. Paul Simon.

Q. Doc's house in *Back to the Future* was actually what historic home in Pasadena?

A. The Gamble House.

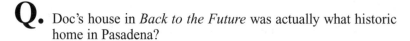

Q. Where is the California State Fair held every August?

A. Sacramento.

Q. What singer-actor who starred in *The Jazz Singer* also popularized the song "California, Here I Come"?

A. Al Jolson.

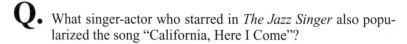

Q. What was the unofficial name of the members of the entertainment industry who were briefly jailed for "contempt of Congress" before the House Un-American Activities Committee?

A. The Hollywood Ten.

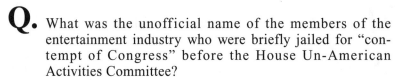

Q. According to the pop song, what is "twenty-six miles across the sea"?

A. Santa Catalina Island.

Q. What surfing-music band lost one member in a drowning accident?

A. The Beach Boys.

Q. Who was thought to be the model for the character of Charles Foster Kane in Orson Welles's film *Citizen Kane*?

A. William Randolph Hearst.

Q. Will Rogers was the mayor of what city?

A. Beverly Hills.

Q. What is the name of the annual event held in Angels Camp that re-creates a famous contest from a Mark Twain story?

A. The Jumping Frog Jubilee.

Q. Jack Benny met his future wife in the hosiery department of which Los Angeles department store?

A. May Company.

Q. *American Graffiti* supposedly took place in what California town?

A. Modesto (also the hometown of the movie's director, George Lucas).

Q. What was the name of Gene Autry's home in Los Angeles County?

A. Melody Ranch.

Q. Bodega Bay was the locale for what Hitchcock thriller?

A. *The Birds.*

Q. The first Academy Awards ceremony was held in what hotel in 1929?

A. Hollywood Roosevelt.

Q. To what ballroom could people take a steamship to dance to the big bands of the 1930s and 1940s?

A. The Casino Ballroom, on Catalina Island.

Q. The giant octopus from *It Came from Beneath the Sea* attacked what city?

A. San Francisco.

Q. Next to Paramount, what was the second-largest Hollywood film company in the 1920s?

A. MGM (Metro-Goldwyn Mayer).

Q. Where can you experience a simulated earthquake in San Francisco?

A. The Planetarium.

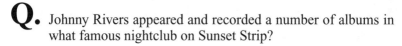

Q. Johnny Rivers appeared and recorded a number of albums in what famous nightclub on Sunset Strip?

A. The Whisky A Go Go.

Q. In what Hollywood hotel did John Belushi die of an overdose in 1982?

A. Chateau Marmont.

Q. What late sixties song was subtitled "Wear Some Flowers in Your Hair"?

A. "San Francisco."

Q. The Monterey Jazz Festival has been held in what month every year since 1957?

A. September.

Q. Where was director Sam Peckinpah born?

A. Fresno.

Q. What classic outdoor amphitheater is located in Griffith Park?

A. The Greek Theatre.

Q. What L. A. group became famous in the mid-1960s with such hits as "Eight Miles High"?

A. The Byrds.

Q. In the film *Lost Horizon*, the setting of Shangri-La was shot where?

A. The Ojai Valley.

Q. Where was Marilyn Monroe born?

A. Los Angeles, in 1926.

Q. What famous guitarist and tie designer was born in San Francisco in 1942?

A. Jerry Garcia.

Q. What year was the fifty-foot-high "Hollywoodland" sign constructed?

A. 1923. (The "land" came off in 1941.)

Q. "California and You" was first recorded in 1914 by what singer?

A. Irving Kaufman.

Q. At what Southern California museum can children ride a police motorcycle, dress up like firemen, and simulate other everyday adult experiences?

A. Los Angeles Children's.

Q. At what oceanside amusement park in California can a person ride a wooden roller coaster and a 1911 carousel?

A. The Santa Cruz Beach Boardwalk.

Q. What nightly Yosemite event was begun in 1872 and occurred for the last time in 1968?

A. The Fire Fall.

Q. Which 1923 Los Angeles hotel has served as a backdrop for more than three hundred films, including *Chinatown*, *The Sting*, and *A Star Is Born*?

A. The Biltmore Los Angeles.

Q. The Mamas and The Papas released "California Dreamin' " in what year?

A. 1966.

Q. Which luxurious lodging doubled as the Saint Gregory Hotel in the TV series *Hotel*?

A. The Fairmont, in San Francisco.

Q. The Institute for the Study of Non-Violence in Carmel was founded by what folk singer?

A. Joan Baez.

Q. Mel Blanc, Clint Eastwood, Bruce Lee, and Natalie Wood all hailed from what city?

A. San Francisco.

Q. What annual October festival features performances of traditional California songs?

A. The Western Regional Folk Festival, in San Francisco.

Q. Where were Lawrence Olivier and Vivien Leigh married?

A. The San Ysidro Ranch, in Montecito.

Q. What was the name of the first Mickey Mouse animated cartoon produced from Disney's studio in Hollywood in 1928?

A. *Plane Crazy.*

Q. What famous singer and guitarist was a native of San Jose?

A. Chuck Berry.

Q. Where can you learn about the history of the brassiere, among other underwear trivia?

A. The Frederick's of Hollywood Lingerie Museum.

Q. What "Surf City" duo lured men to California with the promise of "two girls for every boy"?

A. Jan and Dean.

Q. At which mission were the most suspenseful scenes of *Vertigo* filmed?

A. San Juan Bautista.

Q. Who is the owner of the Mission Ranch, a pastoral country inn in Carmel?

A. Clint Eastwood.

Q. The International Organ Festival and site of one of the world's largest organ installations is located where?

A. Balboa Park, in San Diego.

Q. "San Fernando Valley" was recorded by what famous singer in 1943?

A. Bing Crosby.

Q. Hollywood's cowboy stars are honored at what Los Angeles museum?

A. The Autry Museum of Western Heritage, in Griffith Park.

Q. What served as the 1938 Santa Monica Airport in *The Rocketeer*?

A. The Santa Maria Airport.

Q. The A&M record company in Los Angeles was founded by what two men?

A. Herb Alpert and Jerry Moss.

Q. Where are Errol Flynn, W. C. Fields, and Clark Gable buried?

A. Forest Lawn, in Glendale.

Q. What is the third-largest film festival in North America?

A. The Los Angeles Independent Film Festival. (The top two are the Toronto and Sundance Film Festivals.)

Q. What Fifth Dimension hit of 1969 had obvious ties to the state?

A. "California Soul."

Q. Actor Nicolas Cage is a native of what city?

A. Long Beach.

Q. Singer Connie Francis recorded what song with a California city name in 1961?

A. "Hollywood."

Q. Thurl Ravenscroft narrated the Laguna Beach Pageant of the Masters for twenty years. What other voice role was he famous for?

A. Kellogg's "Tony the Tiger."

Q. What famous actress and animal rights activist co-owns the Cypress Inn in Carmel, where pets are greeted with open arms and dog biscuits?

A. Doris Day.

Q. Who hosts the TV series *California Gold*?

A. Huell Howser.

Q. What is the state song?

A. "I Love You, California."

———∞∞∞———

Q. Los Angeles native Natalie Cole won two Grammy awards in 1991 for what album?

A. *Unforgettable.*

———∞∞∞———

Q. Where is a famous state garlic festival held every year?

A. Gilroy.

———∞∞∞———

Q. At what outdoor spot in Venice Beach can you watch the top bodybuilders in the West lift weights?

A. Muscle Beach.

———∞∞∞———

Q. What was the first radio station in California?

A. KQW in San Jose, established in 1912.

———∞∞∞———

Q. What is the name of the eccentric theater at Death Valley Junction where one-woman ballet and pantomime performances are held?

A. The Amargosa Opera House.

———∞∞∞———

Q. What singer in the Limeliters folk group once owned the counterculture Morningstar Ranch in Sonoma County?

A. Lou Gottlieb.

Q. What was the first commercial television station to go into operation in California in 1947?

A. KTLA, in Los Angeles.

———— ⟨⟩ ————

Q. Who wrote the play *California Suite*?

A. Neil Simon.

———— ⟨⟩ ————

Q. "I Left My Heart in San Francisco" was popularized by what singer?

A. Tony Bennett.

———— ⟨⟩ ————

Q. *Shadow of a Doubt, Pollyanna*, and *Smile* were filmed in what city?

A. Santa Rosa.

———— ⟨⟩ ————

Q. Where is the Roy Rogers–Dale Evans Museum?

A. Victorville.

———— ⟨⟩ ————

Q. What is the name of the whale that stars in Sea World's biggest daily show?

A. Shamu.

———— ⟨⟩ ————

Q. The celebrity footprint-handprint tradition at Grauman's Chinese Theatre began in 1927 when what silent screen star accidentally stepped in a sidewalk of wet cement?

A. Norma Talmadge.

Q. What is the name of the world's tallest and fastest stand-up roller coaster at Six Flags Magic Mountain?

A. Riddler's Revenge.

Q. For nearly ninety years, Newport Beach has hosted what nightly event during the Christmas season?

A. The Boat Parade of Lights.

Q. Where is the *Tonight Show* filmed?

A. NBC Studios in Burbank.

Q. The ranch of what late cowboy star is now a county park near Newhall?

A. William S. Hart.

Q. What Hollywood building was constructed to resemble a stack of records with a needle on top?

A. The Capitol Records Building.

Q. Sacramento hosts a three-day music jubilee each May that focuses on what two types of music?

A. Ragtime and Dixieland.

Q. What theater on Hollywood Boulevard was one of the first art deco movie palaces in the United States?

A. The Pantages Theater.

Q. What Pasadena-born chef first starred in *The French Chef* in 1963 on educational television?

A. Julia Child.

———

Q. The Lawrence Welk Museum is located in what community, also home to the world's largest champagne glass?

A. Escondido.

———

Q. What attraction in Klamath is guarded by giant statues of Paul Bunyan and Babe?

A. The Trees of Mystery.

———

Q. What actress received the first star in the Hollywood Walk of Fame in 1960?

A. Joanne Woodward.

———

Q. What year did Universal Studios offer its first tram tour?

A. 1964.

———

Q. What 1912 theater in San Francisco has hosted James Brown, Jefferson Airplane, and Ike and Tina Turner, and is known as the home of the San Francisco sound?

A. The Fillmore.

———

Q. The Rose Parade was modeled after a similar event in what country?

A. France (in Nice).

Q. What was the first dramatic film shot entirely in Los Angeles?

A. *The Power of the Sultan* (1918).

———— ❦ ————

Q. What year did Moon Unit Zappa record "Valley Girl"?

A. 1982.

———— ❦ ————

Q. Where are the Academy Awards held nearly every year?

A. The Shrine Auditorium.

———— ❦ ————

Q. At what exclusive California spa was the mud bath scene from *The Player* filmed?

A. Two Bunch Palms, in Desert Hot Springs.

———— ❦ ————

Q. What organization owns the largest collection of film-location photographs in the world?

A. The California Film Commission.

———— ❦ ————

Q. As of 1995, how many drive-in theaters remained in California?

A. 135.

———— ❦ ————

Q. At what high school did actor Tom Hanks first perform in a play?

A. Skyline High, in Oakland.

Q. What famous singer attended San Francisco State College, where he set high-jump records?

A. Johnny Mathis.

———

Q. What surf guitarist scored a hit in 1961 with "Let's Go Trippin'"?

A. Dick Dale.

———

Q. What was the first L. A. theater designed for talking motion pictures?

A. The Tower Theater, on Broadway.

———

Q. What year did the groups Santana and Sly and the Family Stone form (in San Francisco)?

A. 1967.

———

Q. Who was crowned California Artichoke Queen by the Kiwanis Club in Watsonville in 1948?

A. Marilyn Monroe.

———

Q. Warner Brothers released the first *Road Runner* cartoon in what year?

A. 1949.

———

Q. What California native starred as Old Ranger in the 1966 TV show *Death Valley Days*?

A. Ronald Reagan.

Q. In what year was the Old Nevada Theater in Nevada City established?

A. 1865.

⸻

Q. What is the name of the long-running, western-themed entertainment show featured daily in Frontierland at Disneyland?

A. *The Golden Horseshoe Revue.*

⸻

Q. What Eagles album won a Grammy Award in 1977?

A. *Hotel California.*

⸻

Q. At what hotel did the "Munchkins" stay while filming *The Wizard of Oz*?

A. The Old Culver City Hotel.

⸻

Q. What is the name of the Fort Bragg-to-Willits rail ride?

A. The Skunk Train.

⸻

Q. Griffith Observatory in Los Angeles features a bronze bust of what actor along its walkway?

A. James Dean. (Scenes from *Rebel Without a Cause* were shot here.)

⸻

Q. The state's first school of cinema and television was founded at what university?

A. USC.

Q. Where can you experience the sense of high-speed time travel, face dinosaurs, and witness a fiery inferno?

A. Universal Studios, Hollywood.

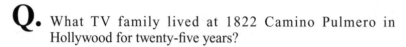

Q. What TV family lived at 1822 Camino Pulmero in Hollywood for twenty-five years?

A. The Nelson family—Ozzie, Harriet, David, and Ricky.

Q. The Hollywood Studio Museum is located in a barn where Cecil B. DeMille directed what 1914 film?

A. *The Squaw Man.*

Q. How many times were the Academy Awards presented in the Coconut Grove of the Ambassador Hotel?

A. Six.

Q. The original 1956 *Invasion of the Body Snatchers* was filmed in the Hollywood Hills and what town's square?

A. Sierra Madre.

Q. In *Star Trek IV*, the scenes of the Sausalito Cetacean Institute were actually filmed where?

A. The Monterey Bay Aquarium.

Q. All of the films shown in Carmel's annual Forest Movie Series have what in common?

A. They're all shot in Monterey County.

Q. The Great American Melodrama and Vaudeville is staged year-round in what little town?

A. Oceano.

———∞———

Q. Oroville hosts what musical event every year in March?

A. The Old Time Fiddlers Contest.

———∞———

Q. In what romantic comedy was there a scene in which Steve Martin was shooting at other motorists?

A. *L. A. Story*.

———∞———

Q. What vegetable does Holtville celebrate every winter at its annual festival?

A. The carrot.

———∞———

Q. What is the oldest African-American-owned and independently funded theater in the nation?

A. The Ebony Showcase, in Los Angeles, established in 1950.

———∞———

Q. The office building at 444 South Flower in downtown Los Angeles is known by what nickname?

A. The *L. A. Law* Building.

———∞———

Q. What mountain in the Tahoe National Forest is named after a famous nineteenth-century femme fatale?

A. Mount Lola (after Lola Montez).

Q. The most extravagant home in Los Angeles, a 123-room chateau larger than the Taj Majal, is owned by what entertainment mogul?

A. Producer Aaron Spelling.

Q. What restaurant chain has become known for its collections of entertainment memorabilia?

A. Planet Hollywood.

Q. Jim Morrison, Francis Ford Coppola, Carol Burnett, Tim Robbins, and conductor John Williams have what in common?

A. All are UCLA alumni.

Q. Where can you go to view the set from the sitcom *Cheers* and the bridge from *Star Trek: The Next Generation*?

A. The Hollywood Entertainment Museum.

Q. What is the highest-grossing, single-screen theater in the nation?

A. El Capitan Theater, in Hollywood.

Q. At the Hollywood Memorial Cemetery, what man known for his famous cartoon voice has an epitaph that reads, "That's All, Folks"?

A. Mel Blanc.

Q. The Queen Anne cottage seen in the opening sequence of *Fantasy Island* is located in what famous gardens?

A. The Los Angeles State and County Arboretum.

Q. *That Thing You Do!*, directed by California native Tom Hanks, was supposed to be set in Erie, Pennsylvania, in 1964, but where was it actually filmed?

A. Downtown Orange, California.

Q. Born Douglas Elton Ulman and Gladys Mary Smith, respectively, what married duo of silent-screen stars called their Beverly Hills mansion "Pickfair"?

A. Douglas Fairbanks and Mary Pickford.

Q. According to a Rodgers and Hammerstein song, what street is in "San Francisco, California, U.S.A"?

A. Grant Avenue.

Q. What L. A. landmark served as Harrison Ford's home in *Blade Runner*?

A. The Bradbury Building.

Q. What seaside town has a Dennis the Menace playground in one of its parks?

A. Monterey.

Q. What Hollywood screenwriter and playwright authored *The Country Girl* for which Grace Kelly won an Oscar?

A. Clifford Odets.

Q. What Hollywood correspondent portrayed herself in the movie *Hollywood Hotel*?

A. Louella Parsons.

Q. What movie star was born in La Jolla, attended the University of California at Berkeley, and won an Academy Award for a 1962 film?

A. Gregory Peck *(To Kill a Mockingbird)*.

Q. California's first theater was started in 1847 by John A. Swan in what town?

A. Monterey.

Q. What annual offbeat Pasadena parade features businessman "briefcase drills" and other farcical forms of entertainment?

A. The Doo Dah Parade.

Q. The Jolly Trolley travels through what "town" at Disneyland?

A. Toontown.

Q. Which famous amphibian was grand marshal of the Pasadena Tournament of Roses Parade?

A. Kermit the Frog.

Q. In what valley were most of the scenes from *ET: The Extraterrestrial* filmed?

A. San Fernando.

Q. What California assemblyman cowrote the film *Attack of the Killer Tomatoes*?

A. Steve Peace.

Q. The opening credits of the soap opera *Santa Barbara* showed what hotel?

A. Four Seasons Biltmore, in Santa Barbara.

Q. The 1981 Academy Award for best director was won by what Santa Monica-born actor?

A. Robert Redford *(Ordinary People)*.

Q. What was California native Bo Derek's original name?

A. Mary Cathleen Collins.

Q. What 1941 movie featured Humphrey Bogart as Mad Dog Earle and Ida Lupino as the moll?

A. *High Sierra.*

Q. Who founded the San Francisco magazine *Rolling Stone* in 1967?

A. Jann Wanner.

Q. What Concord-born pianist and composer founded a famous jazz quartet in 1951?

A. Dave Brubeck.

Q. What San Leandro-born actor starred in *Seahunt?*

A. Lloyd Bridges.

Q. Who sang, "I'm going to see the folks I dig, I'll even kiss a Sunset pig, California, I'm coming home"?

A. Joni Mitchell, in "California," 1971.

Q. Actor Robert Duvall was born in what city?

A. San Diego.

Q. What rock band was formed in San Jose in 1970 and scored their first number-one hit with the song "Black Water"?

A. The Doobie Brothers.

Q. What popular California singer and what state governor were long-time companions?

A. Linda Ronstadt and Jerry Brown.

Q. From the 1930s to the 1960s, nearly four hundred westerns were shot in the rocky hills a few miles west of which Sierra Nevada town?

A. Lone Pine.

Q. What TV series was based on real case files from the L. A. Police Department?

A. *Dragnet.*

Q. An annual accordion festival is hosted by what California town?

A. Cotati.

Q. What was the name of Mr. Drysdale's bank in *The Beverly Hillbillies*?

A. The Commerce Bank of Beverly Hills.

Q. Where did Joe DiMaggio and Marilyn Monroe get married in 1953?

A. San Francisco City Hall.

Q. Although the producers of *90210* are alumni of Beverly Hills High, where was the actual TV series filmed?

A. Torrance High School.

Q. What actor and actress starred in the 1946 western *California*?

A. Ray Milland and Barbara Stanwyck.

Q. According to the theme song, what TV family moved from "West Virginee" to stay in "sunny Californ-i-ay"?

A. *The Real McCoys.*

Q. Frankie Avalon and Annette Funicello's beach movies were all shot at what site?

A. Paradise Cove, in Malibu.

Q. In what county can George Lucas's Skywalker Ranch be found?

A. Marin.

Q. In *Return of the Jedi*, the desert planet of Tatooine was actually shot where?

A. Buttercup Valley, near the California-Arizona border.

Q. The Blair House in Mendocino was used to depict the heroine's home in what TV series?

A. *Murder, She Wrote.*

Q. Where can children encounter Charles Schulz's cartoon characters in Knott's Berry Farm?

A. Camp Snoopy.

Q. What hip character from *77 Sunset Strip* was TV's top teen idol in the late 1950s?

A. Kookie (Edd Byrnes).

Q. Which campy vampire film featured the Santa Cruz Boardwalk?

A. *The Lost Boys.*

Q. What Georgian mansion was used as a film location for the TV series *Dynasty* as well as the films *Heaven Can Wait* and *The Joy Luck Club*?

A. Filoli, in Woodside.

HISTORY

Q. California's first tax-supported public school opened in which city?

A. San Francisco, in 1850.

Q. For what product did Isidore Boudin's bakery become famous in 1850?

A. Sourdough bread.

Q. Who sailed into San Diego Bay in 1542 and claimed the area for Spain?

A. Juan Rodriguez Cabrillo.

Q. What was the target of Owens Valley farmers and their dynamite in 1913?

A. The Los Angeles aqueduct, built to carry water from the Owens Valley.

Q. When was California's public library system founded?

A. 1909.

Q. What was unique about the divorce legislation passed in California in 1969?

A. First no-fault divorce laws in United States.

———⟨∞⟩———

Q. When did California become a state?

A. September 9, 1850, the thirty-first state.

———⟨∞⟩———

Q. What brought about the rapid expansion of aircraft manufacturing in California?

A. World War II.

———⟨∞⟩———

Q. What newly established village had more segments to its name than it had founding families?

A. El Pueblo de Nuestra Senora la Reina de Los Angeles de Porciuncula—said to be founded by eleven families.

———⟨∞⟩———

Q. What Mendocino County town invented its own language called "Boontling" in the 1880s?

A. Boonville.

———⟨∞⟩———

Q. Whose failure at making tents for the forty-niners led him to a riveting alternative?

A. Levi Strauss, with his blue jeans.

———⟨∞⟩———

Q. What city was the first nonmilitary community in California?

A. San Jose, established in 1777.

Q. For four decades, what self-taught horticulturist made Santa Rosa his home?

A. Luther Burbank.

———— ⊗∞ ————

Q. Where did the 1846 Bear Flag Revolt take place?

A. Sonoma.

———— ⊗∞ ————

Q. Who was California's first millionaire?

A. Sam Brannan, builder of Calistoga's hot springs resort.

———— ⊗∞ ————

Q. How long was Death Valley Scotty a member of the *Buffalo Bill Wild West Show*?

A. Twelve years.

———— ⊗∞ ————

Q. The San Francisco Presidio, founded in 1776, remained an active military post until what year?

A. 1994.

———— ⊗∞ ————

Q. The 1906 San Francisco earthquake struck at five o'clock in the morning and lasted how long?

A. Less than a minute, but the resulting fires burned for three days.

———— ⊗∞ ————

Q. California's population growth from 1940 to 1970 averaged how many people per year?

A. Five hundred thousand.

Q. Why was Walt Disney at one time forced to show identification for access to his own studios?

A. After Pearl Harbor, the U.S. Army occupied several large Disney buildings.

Q. What is the smallest national historic site in California?

A. The Eugene O'Neill National Historic Site, in Danville.

Q. What was the name of the road linking the early Spanish missions, presidios, and pueblos from San Diego to Santa Clara?

A. *El Camino Real* (the Royal Road).

Q. Who was the army corporal who served four years as governor of the province of California?

A. Corporal Vincente Felix, who assumed control upon the death of Governor De Neve.

Q. Who was the last Mexican governor of California?

A. Pio Pico.

Q. How was Edward Fitzgerald Beale linked to the Tejon lands north of Los Angeles?

A. He established the first permanent residence there in the 1850s.

Q. Spain rushed settlers to San Diego and Monterey to ward off settlement by whom?

A. The Russians, in 1768.

Q. Benicia served as California's capital for how long?

A. Thirteen months, 1853–54.

Q. What San Francisco mayor was removed from office because of corruption during the reconstruction after the 1906 earthquake?

A. Eugene Schmitz.

Q. What was the immense construction project in Southern California that began in 1899 and reached completion fifteen years later?

A. Los Angeles Harbor.

Q. The group called Indians of All Tribes took over what nationally known installation in 1969 and held it for two years?

A. Alcatraz.

Q. When was Mankoto Hagiwara's Japanese Tea Garden, a gift to San Francisco, created?

A. In 1895.

Q. The 835-acre Beauty Ranch near Glen Ellen was the retreat for what popular author?

A. Jack London.

Q. Did the Native-American population increase or decrease during the Spanish mission period?

A. Decreased by 50 percent, largely because of diseases introduced by the Europeans.

Q. Who was the first black mayor of Los Angeles?

A. Thomas Bradley, elected to his first of five terms in 1973.

―――∞∞∞―――

Q. Who was the highly acclaimed nineteenth-century San Francisco actor whose brother abruptly ended his own acting career in Washington, D.C.?

A. Edwin Booth, brother of John Wilkes Booth.

―――∞∞∞―――

Q. What is the oldest California building still in use?

A. The Chapel–Mission San Juan Capistrano.

―――∞∞∞―――

Q. What Chinese publisher-activist crossed the continent more than eighty times to speak out against discrimination toward immigrants?

A. Ng Poon Chew.

―――∞∞∞―――

Q. It was how long before the news of California's admission to the Union reached the West Coast?

A. Nearly two months.

―――∞∞∞―――

Q. During San Francisco's lawless years, what was the daring gang of Australian robbers called?

A. The Sydney Ducks; they even robbed establishments during business hours.

―――∞∞∞―――

Q. The grizzly bear, now extinct in California, shares its space on the state seal with whom?

A. Minerva, Roman goddess of wisdom, and a miner.

Q. When did the California State Lottery become official?

A. 1986.

———※———

Q. Amadeo Peter Giannini's little Bank of Italy grew to become what bank?

A. Bank of America.

———※———

Q. Who built his own railroad rather than pay the rising rates of the Southern Pacific?

A. John D. "Smokestack" Spreckels built the San Diego and Arizona Railroad, 1919.

———※———

Q. What was the first Spanish expedition to California that included women and children as well as soldiers and missionaries?

A. The Anza overland expedition to San Gabriel, 1774–1776.

———※———

Q. By 1920 most citizens of Los Angeles lived within what distance of a trolley line?

A. Four blocks.

———※———

Q. Who was the first Japanese American elected to the U.S. Senate?

A. S. I. Hayakawa.

———※———

Q. Who took responsibility for the collapse of the Saint Francis Dam north of Los Angeles?

A. William Mulholland, the man who successfully planned the great Los Angeles Aqueduct.

Q. Ancient coastal village sites of the Wintun and Costanoan tribes were often marked by what?

A. Mounds of clam shells that reached as high as twenty feet.

Q. What fort was built north of Los Angeles in the 1850s to guard the Grapevine Pass?

A. Fort Tejon, intended to deter Native-American raiders.

Q. Amended more than 350 times, when was the current state constitution adopted?

A. 1879.

Q. Who was the famous author who courted Fanny Osbourne during his 1879 stay in Monterey?

A. Robert Louis Stevenson.

Q. Who was the Englishman who developed the San Francisco cable car system?

A. Andrew Hallidie, in 1873.

Q. Who was the California woman who helped pass laws in the early twentieth century to regulate wages and working conditions for women and children?

A. Katherine Philips Edson.

Q. How many missions were there in the chain established in California by the Spanish?

A. Twenty-one.

Q. What is the name of the building that was Frank Lloyd Wright's first commission in Los Angeles?

A. Hollyhock House.

———— ∞ ————

Q. Forty-nine of the ninety-one members of what wagon train survived their entrapment by early winter 1846?

A. The Donner party.

———— ∞ ————

Q. Who was the showman who built Mann's Chinese Theater on Hollywood Boulevard in 1927?

A. Sid Grauman.

———— ∞ ————

Q. Where was a temple with chapels for Taoism, Confucianism, and Buddhism built?

A. Oroville, the Chinese Temple, in 1863.

———— ∞ ————

Q. What natural calamity finished the rancheros in their struggle for survival?

A. The great drought of 1860–1865.

———— ∞ ————

Q. The Spanish explorers named the territory "California," but where did they get the name?

A. From a mythical paradise described in Garci Ordonez de Montalvo's book *Las Sergas de Esplandian.*

———— ∞ ————

Q. The daring Pony Express rushed mail from Saint Joseph, Missouri, to what city in about a week?

A. Sacramento. (Mail had previously taken up to four months.)

Q. What former movie star won more votes in 1980 than all of the Oscar candidates combined?

A. Former governor Ronald Reagan, when he was elected president of the United States.

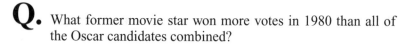

Q. The lawlessness of 1850s San Francisco prompted the formation of what group?

A. The Vigilante Committee, headed by Sam Brannan.

Q. California voters approved what referendum that cut local property taxes by 57 percent?

A. Proposition 13, in 1978.

Q. Who was the Franciscan credited with establishing California's chain of missions?

A. Padre Junipero Serra.

Q. When did Death Valley Scotty's Coyote Special set a new railroad speed record from Los Angeles to Chicago?

A. 1905.

Q. What doll emerged from the Mattel Company in El Segundo in 1959?

A. Barbie.

Q. Lebec, near the summit of Tejon Pass, was once the western headquarters for what?

A. The U.S. Camel Corps.

Q. What was the name of the wooden route that was built over the Algodones Dunes in 1915–16 to improve travel between Phoenix and San Diego?

A. The Plank Road, literally a roadbed covered with wooden planks.

Q. What young entrepreneur joined Steve Wozniak in a home garage to form the Apple Computer Company?

A. Steven Jobs, in 1975.

Q. What native of Yorba Linda rebuilt relations between the United States and China?

A. Richard Nixon, the thirty-seventh president of the United States.

Q. What wealthy Californians were moved by the death of their son to found a university?

A. Mr. and Mrs. Leland Stanford.

Q. Which Native Americans rose up and destroyed two Spanish missions in 1781?

A. The Yumas.

Q. Fort Ross, near Jenner, was built by fur hunters from what nation?

A. Russia.

Q. Cesar Chavez asked grape pickers to strike in 1965, but it was how many years before their battle with the fruit growers was won?

A. Eleven.

Q. At the peak of the rancho period, Californios, the Mexican holders of large land grants, were afforded much free social time by whom?

A. Their Native-American field and ranch hands who did most of the work.

Q. When did the Bidwell-Bartelson train, the first substantial wagon train, reach California?

A. 1841.

Q. When did the strongest Los Angeles earthquake strike, killing sixty-four people?

A. 1971.

Q. The ranch house of Will Rogers, the humorist of the 1930s, is located where?

A. Pacific Palisades.

Q. Lynch mobs swept into which neighborhoods in Los Angeles and San Francisco?

A. The Chinese neighborhoods, in the 1870s.

Q. The Pasadena Freeway, California's first, was built in 1940 and extended how far?

A. Nine miles.

Q. The Santa Clara Valley, famous for its fruit trees, was transformed in the 1970s and 1980s by what tiny manmade object?

A. The silicon chip.

Q. The opening of the Panama Canal in 1914 shortened the sea route between New York and San Francisco from thirteen thousand miles to what distance?

A. Fifty-two hundred miles.

Q. At which mission was the altar painted by an American sailor who had jumped ship?

A. Mission San Juan Bautista.

Q. What highway became the most heavily traveled escape route to California in the 1930s?

A. Route 66 from the Dust Bowl.

Q. A fare war in the late 1880s between the Santa Fe and the Southern Pacific railroads reduced the transcontinental fare to what all-time low amount?

A. One dollar.

Q. High on its perch overlooking the Pacific, the Hearst Castle was a product of what decade?

A. Most of the Spanish-Moorish structure was built in the 1930s.

Q. A powerful man in 1880s San Francisco, who was the publisher of the *San Francisco Chronicle*?

A. Michael DeYoung.

Q. Where was the first tax-supported junior college in the United States established?

A. Fresno, in 1910.

Q. What two events put Los Angeles on the map as a shipping terminal?

A. Completion of Los Angeles Harbor, 1914, and the Panama Canal, 1915.

Q. Who was the state's first commercial wine grower in the 1820s Los Angeles area?

A. Joseph Chapman.

Q. When did Sir Frances Drake drop anchor north of San Francisco Bay?

A. 1579—the English explorer claimed the area for Queen Elizabeth.

Q. Once independent of Spain in 1821, Mexico moved to eliminate whose power over the Native Americans?

A. The California missions.

Q. Beginning in 1910, immigrants arriving in San Francisco were processed where?

A. Angel Island, in San Francisco Bay.

Q. The early explorers of California's coast focused their efforts on locating what cross-continental waterway that would link the Atlantic and Pacific Oceans?

A. The Strait of Anian, a mythical shortcut through North America.

Q. What California valley was once referred to as Starvation Valley?

A. The Tulare Basin of the Central Valley.

Q. How many of the one hundred thousand Japanese Americans who were placed in internment camps in 1942 were American citizens?

A. Approximately two-thirds.

Q. Who was the naturalist who studied and wrote about California wilderness lands and founded the Sierra Club in 1892?

A. John Muir.

Q. What ended the glorious escapades of the Pony Express in 1861?

A. The telegraph.

Q. In the early twentieth century, what Southern California oil field became one of the most productive in the world?

A. Signal Hill, in Long Beach.

Q. Who introduced navel oranges to Southern California?

A. Luther and Eliza Tibbets.

Q. What was the 1965 law that expanded immigration quotas for Asians, among others?

A. The Immigration and Nationality Act.

Q. When did Californian Richard Nixon resign as president of the United States?

A. August 1974.

Q. Why was California's admission into the Union delayed nearly a year by the U.S. Congress?

A. Congress wanted a balance on the slavery issue; California stood against slavery.

———⊗⊗⊗———

Q. What unsuccessful gold miner became a best-selling writer of mining stories?

A. Bret Harte.

———⊗⊗⊗———

Q. When did construction at the western end of the transcontinental railroad begin?

A. In 1863, at Sacramento.

———⊗⊗⊗———

Q. Dry Hole Charlie Woods gained what new nickname in the San Joaquin Valley in March 1910?

A. Gusher Charlie, for bringing in one of the world's largest oil wells near Lakeview.

———⊗⊗⊗———

Q. Who was the delightful Boston girl who captured the hearts of 1852 San Franciscans and was reputed to have sparked the city's culture?

A. Elisa Biscaccianti, a coloratura soprano of world fame.

———⊗⊗⊗———

Q. Figs were introduced as a crop to California by what ethnic group of immigrants?

A. Armenians.

———⊗⊗⊗———

Q. When Sir Francis Drake claimed the land for his queen, he called it what?

A. New Albion.

Q. Who opened McDonald's restaurant in San Bernardino in 1948?

A. Richard and Maurice McDonald.

———∞∞———

Q. Governor John G. Downey sent Hungarian immigrant Agoston Haraszthy back to Europe in the late 1850s for what purpose?

A. To research grape-growing and wine-making procedures, and to select favorable varieties for transplanting in California.

———∞∞———

Q. When the Bear Flag Revolt proclaimed California a republic, what news had yet to arrive?

A. That the Mexican-American War had already begun.

———∞∞———

Q. What type of employment attracted most of the Chinese immigrants in the latter half of the nineteenth century?

A. Jobs in railroad construction.

———∞∞———

Q. Did California gold mining end with the Gold Rush?

A. No; $15–20 million worth of gold is mined each year.

———∞∞———

Q. In the late sixteenth century, Spanish galleons returning to California from the Orient began to fall prey to what English sea captain?

A. Sir Francis Drake.

———∞∞———

Q. California became the nation's most-populous state in what year?

A. 1963.

Q. The San Francisco Conference of 1945 accommodated fifty nations and accomplished what?

A. The formation of the United Nations.

—⟨∞⟩—

Q. What infamous stagecoach robber during Gold Rush days walked to and from his crime scenes, carried an empty shotgun, and left short poems behind?

A. Black Bart, AKA Charles Boles, Charles E. Bolton.

—⟨∞⟩—

Q. What was the designation of the aircraft Chuck Yeager flew beyond the speed of sound in October 1947?

A. The Bell X-1.

—⟨∞⟩—

Q. What U.S. policy assumed that America's expansion to the Pacific was inevitable?

A. Manifest Destiny.

—⟨∞⟩—

Q. What was California's most important crop in 1870?

A. Wheat.

—⟨∞⟩—

Q. When was the Pueblo of Los Angeles founded?

A. September 1781, across the valley from Mission San Gabriel.

—⟨∞⟩—

Q. What writer assisted with her husband's accounts of his explorations of the West?

A. Jessie Benton Frémont, the wife of John Frémont.

Q. Who was Ishi (c. 1860–1916)?

A. The last surviving member of the Yahi tribe.

———∞———

Q. What slave, freed in California in 1855, went on to become a prosperous Los Angeles philanthropist?

A. Biddy Mason, a female slave brought to California from Mississippi.

———∞———

Q. Who discovered the first gold at Sutter's Mill in January 1848?

A. James Wilson Marshall, who had contracted to build Sutter's sawmill.

———∞———

Q. In 1909, what was unique about Earl Gilmore's horse-drawn tank-type vehicle?

A. It was said to be the world's first gas station.

———∞———

Q. California was declared the thirty-first state on September 9, 1850, by what president?

A. Millard Fillmore.

———∞———

Q. What was the treaty that secured the southwestern territories for the United States?

A. The Treaty of Guadalupe Hidalgo.

———∞———

Q. Who ran for governor in 1910 on an anti-railroad platform and served two terms?

A. Hiram Johnson, a feisty lawyer whose theme was "Get the Southern Pacific out of politics!"

Q. When were the Olympic Games first held in California?

A. 1932, in Los Angeles.

—⊗⊗⊗—

Q. What city eventually emerged on the site of New Helvetia (New Switzerland)?

A. Sacramento.

—⊗⊗⊗—

Q. In addition to the panning and hydraulic methods, what was another gold-mining technique?

A. The rocker method.

—⊗⊗⊗—

Q. In 1943, President Roosevelt sent an official representative to Los Angeles to ease tensions between servicemen stationed in the area and what group of locals?

A. Zoot Suiters.

—⊗⊗⊗—

Q. The "Big Four" in California history refers to whom?

A. Charles Crocker, Mark Hopkins, Collis P. Huntington, and Leland Stanford—the railroad kings.

—⊗⊗⊗—

Q. Who turned from unsuccessful gold mining to candy making during the Gold Rush?

A. Domingo Ghirardelli.

—⊗⊗⊗—

Q. California's grape crop was nearly destroyed in 1874 by what?

A. *Phylloxera*, a plant louse.

Q. Early explorers had to be awestruck by the size of what bird?

A. The California condor, with its nine-foot wingspan.

Q. Who claimed the $5,000 reward in 1853 for allegedly killing the famous bandit Joaquin Murieta?

A. Captain John Love of the Rangers, though there were doubts about Murieta's very existence.

Q. What entrepreneur amassed property in Gold Rush country before the strike and lost it all because of the strike?

A. John Sutter, whose property was overrun by miners and settlers.

Q. What mineral, once moved about by twenty-mule teams, is provided exclusively by California?

A. The uncommon mineral boron, which is so common in kitchen cleansers.

Q. What was the first commercial film made in California?

A. *The Count of Monte Cristo,* made in the Los Angeles area in 1907.

Q. What is the small Coachella Valley desert animal that came close to extinction in the 1970s?

A. The fringe-toed lizard, which runs on the sand and also swims through it like a fish in water.

Q. What was Hangtown known as, prior to the lynching from which it got its name?

A. Old Dry Diggings.

Q. What Californio formed a battalion that distinguished itself in the Civil War?

A. Andres Pico.

Q. Where did Philip Armour (meat-packing company), John Studebaker (automobile manufacturer), and Collis P. Huntington (Southern Pacific Railroad) all begin their rise to fame and fortune?

A. The mining town of Placerville.

Q. As foreign traders came to California in the early nineteenth century, they bartered principally for what products?

A. Cattle hides and tallow.

Q. What famous airplane was built by the small Ryan Aircraft Company of San Diego in the 1920s?

A. The *Spirit of St. Louis.*

Q. When did California's second-largest earthquake of the 1900s strike the San Francisco area?

A. October 17, 1989.

Q. Who formed the Central Pacific Railroad Company, organized its backers, and gained government support, but was eventually forced out by the Big Four?

A. Theodore Judah.

Q. Who was California's first governor?

A. Peter H. Burnett.

Q. What was unusual about the Seven Cities of Cíbola, for which the Spanish explorers searched?

A. They were said to have streets paved with gold and silver.

———— ∞∞ ————

Q. Who was a leader of the Bear Flag Revolt who later served as the president of California's constitutional convention?

A. Robert Semple.

———— ∞∞ ————

Q. When did the city of Los Angeles take the state's lead in population away from San Francisco?

A. In 1920, with over a half-million people.

———— ∞∞ ————

Q. What was the last act of James Casey, a San Francisco politician who was accused of corruption?

A. He killed his accuser, reporter James King, and was, in turn, lynched by vigilantes.

———— ∞∞ ————

Q. What object found a place on the California state flag in 1911 with a grizzly bear?

A. A red star.

———— ∞∞ ————

Q. What are the five cities that served as temporary capitals of California between 1850 and 1854?

A. Monterey, San Jose, Vallejo, Benicia, and San Francisco.

———— ∞∞ ————

Q. At their peak during World War II, the Kaiser shipyards in Richmond took how long to build a 10,000-ton liberty ship?

A. Three-and-a-half days—the parts were sequentially numbered.

Q. Born in the early 1960s, what is BART?

A. The Bay Area Rapid Transit.

———— ∞ ————

Q. Who were California's first winemakers?

A. Spanish missionaries.

———— ∞ ————

Q. What was the purpose of the Gentlemen's Agreement of 1908?

A. To limit the entry of Japanese laborers.

———— ∞ ————

Q. When was the state seal of California adopted?

A. 1849.

———— ∞ ————

Q. During the brief period of Mexican control over California, land grants were dispensed freely according to hand-drawn maps that were called what?

A. *Disenos.*

———— ∞ ————

Q. Who was the first person from the United States to journey by land to California?

A. Jedediah Smith, a trapper, 1826.

———— ∞ ————

Q. After his court-martial by the army, what prominent explorer of California went on to serve the Southwest in numerous capacities until 1883?

A. John Frémont.

Q. What two California oil men founded the company that eventually became Union Oil Company?

A. Walter Hardison and Lyman Stewart.

Q. When was Yosemite National Park established?

A. 1890.

Q. John Studebaker, of later automobile fame, began by making and selling what to the miners?

A. Wheelbarrows.

Q. What famous writer was banished from San Francisco for his "politically incorrect" sense of humor?

A. Samuel Clemens, AKA Mark Twain, in the early 1860s.

Q. Of the twenty-three million cars owned by Americans in 1929, how many belonged to Californians?

A. Two million.

Q. What did the early Spanish explorers call that portion of California above Baja?

A. *Alta California.*

Q. In 1842, Commander Jones, U.S.N., believing war with Mexico had begun, mistakenly captured which community?

A. Monterey. (When apprised of his error, he apologized and left.)

Q. Who was the first woman to serve as chief justice of the California Supreme Court?

A. Rose Elizabeth Bird, in 1977.

———∞———

Q. What man, regarded by some as a lunatic, made millions of dollars from San Francisco real estate, began the fruit industry in the Santa Clara Valley, financed a famous observatory, and then literally gave away the remainder of his fortune?

A. James Lick.

———∞———

Q. California oil fields produced how much oil per day at their peak?

A. More than one million barrels.

———∞———

Q. How was California shown on maps in the early 1600s?

A. Father Ascension depicted the territory as an island; the concept lasted more than one hundred years.

———∞———

Q. The Russian-American Company was represented in its explorations and settlements by whom?

A. Nikolai Rezanov; engaged to the daughter of a Californio, he was killed in a riding accident.

———∞———

Q. Father Serra referred to himself as what?

A. The Gray Ox.

———∞———

Q. What California law of the 1930s was declared unconstitutional by the U.S. Supreme Court?

A. The Great Depression Era law closing California's borders to the poor.

Q. What California phenomenon of the 1960s spread worldwide in a decade?

A. Skateboarding.

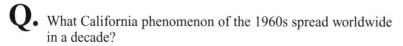

Q. What major shipping channel was opened in 1963?

A. The Sacramento–to–San Francisco Bay channel.

Q. Who was the president at the time of the American acquisition of California?

A. James Polk.

Q. What two brothers from Modesto began their winemaking business in 1933?

A. Ernest and Julio Gallo.

Q. Throughout California, exuberant celebrations each May 5 mark what anniversary?

A. *Cinco de Mayo*, the celebration of Mexican victory at the Battle of Puebla, May 5, 1821.

Q. What was the original name of the town that became San Francisco?

A. Yerba Buena.

Q. The Bay Bridge, built in 1936, links what two cities?

A. San Francisco and Oakland.

Q. Who were the two brothers who founded a major aircraft company in Burbank?

A. Allan and Malcolm Loughhead founded what became Lockheed Aircraft Company.

Q. What U.S. city led the country in gold production until the Gold Rush in California?

A. Charlotte, North Carolina.

Q. What Democratic politician was assassinated in Los Angeles as he campaigned for his party's presidential nomination?

A. Robert Kennedy, in 1968.

Q. What threw California's booming economy into a recession in the early 1970s?

A. Severe cutbacks in military spending.

Q. When were the first offshore oil wells drilled near the California coast?

A. 1896.

Q. What American general, a veteran of the War of 1812, became a leader in the war with Mexico?

A. Stephen Kearny.

Q. Who was the black rights activist of the 1960s acquitted of complicity in murder?

A. Angela Davis.

Q. A member of the counterculture of late 1960s San Francisco was called what?

A. Hippie.

———⚬———

Q. In 1977, another California first was the installation of what?

A. The first fiber-optic cable.

———⚬———

Q. Governor Hiram Johnson ran as vice-presidential candidate on the Progressive Party ticket in 1912 with whom?

A. Teddy Roosevelt. (They lost.)

———⚬———

Q. Who was the Chinese-American woman who helped recruit many of the Flying Tigers for China's air force and who instigated the creation of the U.S. Navy's WAVES?

A. Dr. Margaret Chung. One of eleven children, she worked her way through medical school.

———⚬———

Q. What was the first American sailing ship to reach California in 1796?

A. The *Otter*.

———⚬———

Q. In what two-year period did California's population jump from fifteen thousand to one hundred thousand people?

A. 1848–49.

———⚬———

Q. While many attributed California's major depression of the 1870s to too much wealth in the hands of too few, many laborers blamed what other faction?

A. The cheap, hard-working Chinese laborers who were no longer needed on the Transcontinental Railroad.

Q. What was the site of the first Spanish land grant, Rancho San Rafael, in 1784?

A. Glendale.

Q. California provided how much of the world's oil in 1925?

A. More than one-fifth.

Q. What city in Los Angeles County was known as Clearwater until 1949?

A. Paramount.

Q. What was the western terminus of the Santa Fe Trail?

A. Lexington, renamed El Monte in 1868.

Q. Who was elected governor in 1966 for his first of two terms?

A. Ronald Reagan.

Q. Where was the state's first newspaper published?

A. In Monterey, in 1846.

Q. Joseph Reddeford Walker, Kit Carson, and Ewing Young played what role in California history?

A. They were leading trappers and explorers who followed Jedediah Smith overland to California.

Q. What city, founded by Quakers in 1887, was named for a famous poet?

A. Whittier, for John Greenleaf Whittier.

Q. The new constitution of 1879 was marked by stiffer provisions for regulating what two groups?

A. The railroads and the Chinese immigrants.

Q. What novelist, a Democrat, lost in his 1934 bid for governor, despite over a million supporters for his EPIC (End Poverty in California) program?

A. Upton Sinclair.

Q. Why were Union Army troops stationed on Catalina Island during the Civil War?

A. To prevent southern sympathizers from using it as a base for pirate activities against the North.

Q. What California event served as a major prompt to the Monroe Doctrine in 1823?

A. The threat of Russian expansion at Fort Ross.

Q. What acting secretary of war established the U.S. Naval Academy at Annapolis and served as a principal figure in the occupation of California and the initiation of the Mexican War?

A. George Bancroft.

Q. What Rudy Gernreich design greeted the public in Southern California in 1969?

A. The topless bathing suit.

ARTS & LITERATURE

Q. What humorist wrote, "The coldest winter I ever spent was a summer in San Francisco"?

A. Mark Twain.

Q. Martha Graham, who greatly influenced twentieth-century modern dance, grew up in what town?

A. Santa Barbara.

Q. Who founded the California Institute of the Arts, in Valencia?

A. Walt Disney.

Q. What writer said of Oakland, "There is no *there* there"?

A. Gertrude Stein.

Q. What library in the San Gabriel Valley contains a Gutenberg Bible and one of the finest rare-book collections of Shakespeare?

A. Huntington.

Q. Some of the most original furniture designs of the twentieth century were created by what California husband-and-wife designer team?

A. Charles and Ray Eames.

Q. What was the nickname of famed ceramist Beatrice Wood, who lived in Ojai until the age of 105?

A. The Mama of Dada.

Q. What Pulitzer Prize-winning California newspaper is named after an insect?

A. The *Sacramento Bee*.

Q. More than two hundred outdoor murals are found in what San Francisco neighborhood?

A. The Mission District.

Q. Where along the California coast did author Henry Miller live for eighteen years?

A. Big Sur.

Q. Which San Francisco poet was selected to present a poem for President Clinton's 1993 inauguration?

A. Maya Angelou.

Q. The world's highest-funded art collections are found at which museum?

A. The Getty, in Los Angeles.

Q. What 1876 California hotel is known for its catacombs, gargoyles, and rooftop state symbols, among other architectural oddities?

A. The Mission Inn, in Riverside.

Q. What was the name of writer Jack London's twelve-thousand-square foot house on his Beauty Ranch, which burned down a few days before he was to move in?

A. Wolf House.

Q. California writer Zane Grey published *Riders of the Purple Sage* in what year?

A. 1912.

Q. What are the state's two oldest universities, dating to 1851?

A. Santa Clara University and University of the Pacific.

Q. What Los Angeles work of art was built from backyard junk by laborer Simon Rodia?

A. The Watts Towers.

Q. What was the first and most famous book written by Oakland native Amy Tan?

A. *The Joy Luck Club.*

Q. Photographer Ansel Adams made his first trip to Yosemite National Park in what year?

A. 1916.

Q. One of John Muir's books related his travels in Alaska with his dog Stickeen, but more people remember his writings about what national park?

A. Yosemite.

Q. Lotta's Fountain in San Francisco is a memorial to what turn-of-the-century opera star?

A. Luisa Tetrazzini.

Q. Poet Robinson Jeffers's stone house, High Tor, still stands in what coastal town?

A. Carmel.

Q. What Southern California college is home to paintings by two great muralists, José Orozco and Rico Lebrun?

A. Pomona.

Q. What Nobel Laureate and 1930s Hollywood resident wrote the screenplay for *To Have and Have Not*?

A. William Faulkner.

Q. The Los Angeles Philharmonic first performed at the Hollywood Bowl in what year?

A. 1922.

Q. Which two painters offered the American public some of the first grand views of Yosemite National Park?

A. Albert Bierstadt and Thomas Hill.

Q. Oakland's Jack London first won fame with his stories about the gold rush in what state?

A. Alaska.

Q. To what city was H. L. Mencken referring when he described it as "nineteen suburbs in search of a metropolis"?

A. Los Angeles.

Q. What Pulitzer Prize-winning California poet wrote *Turtle Island* in 1974?

A. Gary Snyder.

Q. What Southern California hotel features an historic covered footbridge on which forty mural scenes of state landmarks have been painted with accompanying verses?

A. The Ritz-Carlton Huntington Hotel, in Pasadena. (The murals were painted by Frank Montague Moore in the 1930s and the verses were written by poet Donald Blanding.)

Q. What novelist wrote *The Octopus*, a fictionalized story of the railroad barons who monopolized California businesses?

A. Frank Norris.

Q. In terms of circulation, what newspaper ranks second in California behind the *Los Angeles Times*?

A. The *San Francisco Chronicle*.

Q. Who was the architect of Hearst Castle?

A. Julia Morgan.

Q. Writer Joan Didion is a native of what town?

A. Sacramento.

Q. What was the name of the fictional family who migrated to California in search of a better life in John Steinbeck's *The Grapes of Wrath*?

A. The Joads.

Q. What famous architect designed a home in the Hollywood Hills for silent-screen star Ramon Navarro?

A. Lloyd Wright (son of Frank Lloyd Wright).

Q. What famous opera tenor happened to be in San Francisco during the 1906 earthquake and vowed never to return to that city?

A. Enrico Caruso.

Q. For what newspaper did California writer Ambrose Bierce work at the turn of the century?

A. The *San Francisco Examiner*.

Q. Other than the Drama and Dance fountain at the Hollywood Bowl, what statue did George Stanley design?

A. The Oscar.

Q. What prestigious school of music and the arts is located in a little town in the San Jacinto Mountains?

A. The Idyllwild Arts Academy.

Q. What Central Valley writer penned *The Human Comedy*, which was made into a movie starring Mickey Rooney?

A. William Saroyan.

Q. What Sacramento museum bears the name of one of California's "Big Four" railroad magnates?

A. Crocker Art.

Q. What Helen Hunt Jackson story is brought to life every year in an outdoor theater pageant in Hemet?

A. *Ramona.*

Q. Where would you go to see the San Francisco Opera perform on opening night?

A. The War Memorial Opera House.

Q. What is the name of the Art Moderne building, on South Central Avenue in Los Angeles, which resembles a red and white ship?

A. The Coca-Cola Bottling Company.

Q. What is the name of Bret Harte's Gold Rush-based short story?

A. "The Luck of Roaring Camp."

Q. What was the biggest market for the first literary journals in California?

A. The mining camps.

Q. What style of painting distinguished the art colony of Laguna Beach in the 1920s?

A. Plein air.

Q. What was the name of Jessamyn West's 1960 novel about unscrupulous real estate promotion in Orange County?

A. *South of the Angels.*

Q. The poet Joaquin Miller was one of the first members of what exclusive men's organization that meets annually in a redwood grove north of San Francisco?

A. The Bohemian Club.

Q. What Pasadena art museum was founded by a multimillion-aire who made an unsuccessful bid for the U.S. Senate and was married to actress Jennifer Jones?

A. The Norton Simon Museum.

Q. The leadership in jazz trends from the 1930s on came primarily from what area?

A. Los Angeles, particularly because of the movie and recording studios there.

Q. What architect designed the contemporary Hyatt Regency in San Francisco and the Bonaventure in Los Angeles?

A. John Portman.

Q. What famous classical pianist-composer said, "The only way to avoid Hollywood is to live there"?

A. Igor Stravinsky.

Q. Which magazine, founded in 1852, first published California's major writers?

A. *Golden Era.*

Q. What author from Alameda became famous for her children's stories about growing up Japanese American?

A. Yoshiko Uchida.

Q. Some people believe that Robert Louis Stevenson's island descriptions in *Treasure Island* were modeled after what stretch of California coastline?

A. Point Lobos State Reserve.

Q. What renowned Scottish-born artist lived in Berkeley and was known for his paintings of the oak trees on the UC campus?

A. William Keith.

Q. What brother architects with a "colorful" last name designed popular craftsman-style homes in the early 1900s?

A. Henry Mather Greene and Charles Sumner Greene.

Q. What Californian wrote the book *Six Crises* in 1962?

A. Richard Nixon.

Q. Which California town is named after the author of *Two Years Before the Mast*?

A. Dana Point, after author Richard Henry Dana.

Q. What Southern California cemetery boasts a huge copy of Leonardo DaVinci's painting *The Last Supper*?

A. Forest Lawn.

━━━━━━━━━━

Q. *Angle of Repose* was written by what Pulitzer Prize-winning novelist and former Stanford professor in 1971?

A. Wallace Stegner.

━━━━━━━━━━

Q. What building is home to the San Francisco Symphony?

A. Davies Hall.

━━━━━━━━━━

Q. What progressive jazz band gained early fame with its performances at Balboa Pavilion?

A. The Stan Kenton Band.

━━━━━━━━━━

Q. Which book, published in 1852, was filled with Mark Twain's descriptions of California life?

A. *Roughing It.*

━━━━━━━━━━

Q. Christo, a landscape artist, is famous for his acres of yellow umbrellas near Fort Tejon. What other display did he install along the Sonoma Coast in 1976?

A. *Running Fence.*

━━━━━━━━━━

Q. What San Francisco bookstore was the main meeting place for Beat era writers such as Jack Kerouac and Henry Miller?

A. City Lights Book Store, owned by poet Lawrence Ferlinghetti.

Q. What photographer became known for her grim, realistic portrayals of the farm families who migrated from the Dust Bowl to California?

A. Dorothea Lange.

———⨍⨍⨍———

Q. Famed lawyer Clarence Darrow defended union organizers in the bombing of what California newspaper's offices?

A. The *Los Angeles Times*.

———⨍⨍⨍———

Q. In what city does the South Coast Repertory perform?

A. Costa Mesa.

———⨍⨍⨍———

Q. Mark Twain first gained national recognition with a short story that featured a California county in the title. What was that story?

A. "The Celebrated Jumping Frog of Calaveras County."

———⨍⨍⨍———

Q. The doors of what San Francisco church are copied from Ghiberti's bronze doors on the baptistry of the cathedral in Florence?

A. Grace Cathedral.

———⨍⨍⨍———

Q. The Californio, Maria Amparo Ruiz de Burton, used what pen name for her book, *The Squatter and the Don*, in 1885?

A. C. Royal. Unable to get it published in her own name, she chose the pseudonym.

———⨍⨍⨍———

Q. What sculptor designed the California Scenario garden in Costa Mesa?

A. Isamu Noguchi.

Q. Which San Francisco hotel features guest rooms that are custom-designed by artist Gary Wyland, Grateful Dead's Jerry Garcia, and Joe Boxer of underwear fame?

A. Hotel Triton.

Q. Fresno native William Saroyan turned down a Pulitzer Prize for what 1939 novel?

A. *The Time of Your Life.*

Q. Where did Eugene O'Neill live for seven years while he wrote *Long Day's Journey into Night* and *The Iceman Cometh*?

A. The Tao House, in Danville.

Q. What is the oldest ballet company in the United States?

A. The San Francisco Ballet.

Q. What California science fiction writer also created the screenplay for the film version of *Moby Dick*?

A. Ray Bradbury.

Q. What is the most widely read English-language poetry publication in the world?

A. *Poetry Flash*, published in San Francisco.

Q. Which Southern California hotel is said to have provided the inspiration for the Emerald City to L. Frank Baum when he wrote *The Wizard of Oz*?

A. Hotel Del Coronado.

Q. What popular novelist based *The Last Tycoon* on his 1930s interlude in Hollywood writing screenplays?

A. F. Scott Fitzgerald.

———✖———

Q. What is San Diego's oldest continuously published newspaper?

A. The *San Diego Union*.

———✖———

Q. What Californian was awarded the Pulitzer Prize for editorial cartooning in 1984?

A. Paul Conrad.

———✖———

Q. When was California author John Steinbeck awarded the Nobel Prize for Literature?

A. 1962.

———✖———

Q. What town south of Eureka has the best preserved Victorian architecture in the state?

A. Ferndale.

———✖———

Q. Raymond Chandler lived where when he wrote the novel *Lady of the Lake* during the 1940s?

A. Brentwood.

———✖———

Q. What is the name of the Big Sur hotel that is famous for its eco-architecture, featuring tree houses, sod-roofed cottages, and a "Butterfly House"?

A. Post Ranch Inn, designed by Micky Meunnig.

Q. Where is the largest university library in the state?

A. University of California at Berkeley.

Q. What museum offers bus tours of the best signs in Los Angeles?

A. The Museum of Neon Art.

Q. What 1969 novel won Laguna Beach author Theodore Taylor a half-dozen literary awards and was made into a movie?

A. *The Cay.*

Q. How many panes of stained glass are in the domed ceiling of the Sheraton Palace Hotel in San Francisco?

A. Eighty thousand.

Q. San Francisco's 1924 art museum, the Legion of Honor, was modeled after a similar building in what city?

A. Paris.

Q. The word "beatniks" was coined by what San Francisco columnist in 1958?

A. Herb Caen.

Q. Dancer Isadora Duncan, novelist Irving Stone, and poet Robert Frost were all natives of what city?

A. San Francisco.

Q. According to circulation figures, where does the Sunday edition of the *Los Angeles Times* rank nationally?

A. Second, behind the *New York Times*.

———— ❧ ————

Q. In his 1968 book *The Pump House Gang*, what author wrote, "Southern California, I found, is a veritable paradise of statuspheres"?

A. Tom Wolfe.

———— ❧ ————

Q. The Pacific Conservatory of the Performing Arts is based in what city?

A. Santa Maria.

———— ❧ ————

Q. What writer and member of the UC Berkeley faculty won the 1980 Nobel Prize for Literature?

A. Czeslaw Milosz.

———— ❧ ————

Q. What is the name of the 150-foot desert figure that was engraved out of the soil by ancestors of the Yuma Indians around 1700?

A. The Blythe Intaglio.

———— ❧ ————

Q. The home of what California author is now a hotel on Catalina Island?

A. Zane Grey.

———— ❧ ————

Q. What is the oldest museum in California?

A. The M. H. de Young Memorial Museum, in San Francisco.

Q. What distinguished California artist painted *The Pageant of History in Northern California?*

A. Millard Sheets.

⸺

Q. The Highland Park home of what noted author and poet was a cultural center of Southern California in the 1900s?

A. Charles Fletcher Lummis.

⸺

Q. What is the oldest private coed university in the West?

A. The University of Southern California, founded in 1876.

⸺

Q. Dashiell Hammett published *The Maltese Falcon* in what year?

A. 1930.

⸺

Q. What landmark building was constructed on Broadway in Los Angeles in 1893?

A. The Bradbury Building.

⸺

Q. What was Nathanael West's 1939 novel that sketched a surreal Hollywood?

A. *The Day of the Locust.*

⸺

Q. "East is East, and West is San Francisco," was written by what noted author in the early 1900s?

A. O. Henry.

Q. Philip Johnson designed what theatrical auditorium for Robert Schuller's Garden Grove Community Church?

A. The Crystal Cathedral.

━━━⟨∞⟩━━━

Q. *Sunset* magazine was founded in what year?

A. 1898.

━━━⟨∞⟩━━━

Q. The former Bullock's Wilshire is one of the finest examples of what type of architecture in Southern California?

A. Art deco.

━━━⟨∞⟩━━━

Q. What California town is the model for Santa Theresa in Sue Grafton's novels?

A. Santa Barbara.

━━━⟨∞⟩━━━

Q. What was the Woody Herman Band's 1940s classic adaptation of rhythm and blues form?

A. The "Woodchoppers' Ball."

━━━⟨∞⟩━━━

Q. Where can you find Hobbiton, USA, a nature walk that pays tribute to *The Hobbit* by J. R. R. Tolkien?

A. Phillipsville.

━━━⟨∞⟩━━━

Q. In Oakland's Jack London Square, what site was a favorite haunt of the author?

A. Heinold's First and Last Chance Saloon.

Q. The main character in John Steinbeck's *Cannery Row* was modeled after what real-life marine biologist?

A. "Doc" Edward Ricketts.

⸻

Q. What are the three theaters at the Music Center in Los Angeles?

A. The Dorothy Chandler Pavilion, Mark Taper Forum, and Ahmanson Theatre.

⸻

Q. California detective writer Erle Stanley Gardner was the creator of what fictional lawyer?

A. Perry Mason.

⸻

Q. What poet laureate wrote *The Mission Play*, popularizing a 1920s revival of the mission period style?

A. John Steven McGroarty.

⸻

Q. Lloyd Wright designed what striking glass and redwood structure in Rancho Palos Verdes?

A. The Wayfarer's Chapel.

⸻

Q. What is the last remaining structure of the 1915 Panama-Pacific Exposition in San Francisco?

A. The Palace of Fine Arts.

⸻

Q. What opera soprano graduated from Mills College in 1876 and eventually adopted a "state" name?

A. Emma Nevada.

Q. What publication became California's first daily newspaper?

A. *Alta California.*

Q. What California architect designed both the Los Angeles Museum of Art and San Francisco's pyramid-shaped Transamerica Building?

A. William Pereira.

Q. What grandniece of Harriet Beecher Stowe lived mainly in Pasadena and was a writer and leader in women's movements?

A. Charlotte Perkins.

Q. What native Californian, who was also mute, sculpted a statue of Padre Serra in San Francisco's Golden Gate Park?

A. Douglas Tilden.

Q. What opera baritone, born in Bakersfield, debuted at New York's Metropolitan Opera in 1923?

A. Lawrence Tibbett.

Q. What is the fictitious San Francisco address of Mrs. Madrigal's apartment house in *Tales of the City*, by Armistead Maupin?

A. Twenty-eight Barbary Lane.

Q. What is the popular name of a La Jolla author and illustrator who wrote *The Seven Lady Godivas*?

A. Dr. Seuss.

Q. What California town's name, when spelled backwards, is a form of poetry?

A. Ukiah.

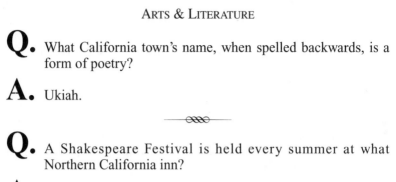

Q. A Shakespeare Festival is held every summer at what Northern California inn?

A. The Benbow Inn.

Q. What British author of *Brave New World* lived his last years in Los Angeles?

A. Aldous Huxley.

Q. In San Francisco, what does "A.C.T." stand for?

A. American Conservatory Theatre.

Q. What is the best-known art form of the Pomo Indians of Northern California?

A. Basketry.

Q. In "Song of the Redwood Tree," what American poet wrote: "The flashing and gold pageant of California, the sudden and gorgeous drama, the sunny and ample lands—"?

A. Walt Whitman.

Q. Renowned photographer Ansel Adams wrote the script for what Christmas Day event held annually at the Ahwahnee in Yosemite Valley?

A. The Bracebridge Dinner.

Q. In what town is Humboldt State University?

A. Arcata.

———— ∞ ————

Q. Who promised artist Thomas Hill $50,000 for his painting of the Transcontinental Railroad, *Driving the Last Spike*, but then refused to buy it?

A. Leland Stanford.

———— ∞ ————

Q. In "Autumn in California," what poet wrote "Autumn in California is a mild and anonymous season"?

A. Kenneth Rexroth.

———— ∞ ————

Q. What novel, written by Robert Louis Stevenson in 1883, described his California adventures near Mount Saint Helena?

A. *The Silverado Squatters.*

———— ∞ ————

Q. What central California town hosts a Mozart Festival every summer?

A. San Luis Obispo.

———— ∞ ————

Q. What famous photography school is situated in the foothills above Santa Barbara?

A. The Brooks Institute.

———— ∞ ————

Q. How old was William Randolph Hearst when he was given control of the *San Francisco Examiner*?

A. Twenty-three.

Q. *California Gold* was painted by what California Impressionist in 1924?

A. William Wendt.

Q. To what town was Joan Didion referring when she wrote, "I had not before 1971 and will probably not again live in a place with a Chevrolet named after it"?

A. Malibu.

Q. What is the name of the ecological community on the Northern California coastline that architect Charles Moore designed?

A. Sea Ranch.

Q. The mission-style Bowers Museum of Cultural Art is located in what city?

A. Santa Ana.

Q. What was the first women's college in the West?

A. Mills College, founded in 1871 as a ladies' seminary.

Q. What artist painted *Sunday Morning in the Mines* and other portraits of California pioneer life?

A. Charles Christian Nahl.

Q. What C. Y. Lee novel of Chinese Americans in San Francisco was later made into a movie?

A. *The Flower Drum Song.*

Q. Where is the Playboy Jazz Festival held every year?

A. The Hollywood Bowl.

───── ∞ ─────

Q. Sculptureland, a twenty-acre park of more than two hundred contemporary sculptures, is situated in what desert town?

A. La Quinta.

───── ∞ ─────

Q. After they were published in England in the 1950s, whose poems were seized by the San Francisco customs office on the grounds that they were obscene?

A. Allen Ginsberg.

───── ∞ ─────

Q. Whittier College was founded by what religious group in 1901?

A. Quakers.

───── ∞ ─────

Q. In her 1980 book *Destinations*, what novelist described Hollywood as "the Versailles of Los Angeles"?

A. Jan Morris.

───── ∞ ─────

Q. In 1903, Andrew Carnegie awarded what town $125,000 to help build a historical museum-library?

A. Petaluma.

───── ∞ ─────

Q. What famous nineteenth-century English writer said, "The mountains of California are so gigantic that they are not favorable to art or poetry"?

A. Oscar Wilde.

Q. The Kern County Board of Supervisors and Associated Farmers tried to ban what book upon its publication in 1939?

A. *The Grapes of Wrath*, by John Steinbeck.

Q. *Land of Sunshine*, an idyllic scene of the Southern California landscape, was painted by what California Impressionist?

A. Maurice Braun.

Q. What state park features the Mountain Theater, in which springtime plays have been performed since 1913?

A. Mount Tamalpais.

Q. *Californians*, published in 1916, was a volume of poems written by what distinguished Carmel poet?

A. Robinson Jeffers.

Q. After the New York Metropolitan, what is the second-oldest continuous opera group in the United States?

A. The San Francisco Opera Company, founded in 1923.

Q. The world's first glass skyscraper, the Hallidie Building in San Francisco, was designed by what architect in 1918?

A. Willis Polk.

Q. "The Celebrated Jumping State of California" was one of many short stories written by what writer?

A. William Saroyan.

Q. The California Impressionists earned what nickname because of their tendency for painting a particular kind of tree?

A. The Eucalyptus School.

Q. With the 1941 publication of his book *Storm*, what UC Berkeley professor popularized the practice of giving storms the names of women?

A. George R. Stewart.

Q. Whose travel literature, including *California Romantic and Beautiful*, contributed to the state's population boom at the turn of the century?

A. George Wharton James.

Q. The first tableau vivant produced by the Laguna Beach Pageant of the Masters in 1932 was what work of art?

A. *Mona Lisa*.

Q. In addition to *Cannery Row*, John Steinbeck wrote what other novel about the Monterey waterfront?

A. *Sweet Thursday*, written in 1954.

Q. Which half-mile mural, located in North Hollywood, is said to be the world's largest?

A. The Tujunga Wash Mural.

Q. Who created Los Angeles detective Philip Marlowe with *The Big Sleep* in 1939?

A. Raymond Chandler.

Q. What Melrose Avenue building in West Hollywood was nicknamed the "Blue Whale" when it was first built in 1975?

A. The Pacific Design Center.

———

Q. What city was Vachel Lindsay writing about in his 1923 poem "The City that Will Not Repent"?

A. San Francisco.

———

Q. The jazz style of the 1950s, combining small groups, complex harmonies, and improvisation, was called what?

A. West Coast Jazz.

———

Q. What two former presidents have presidential libraries in California?

A. Richard Nixon and Ronald Reagan.

———

Q. *The Last Days of the Late, Great State of California* was written by what author in 1968?

A. Curt Gentry.

———

Q. What popular nineteenth-century writer went to Mexico to seek Pancho Villa and disappeared?

A. Ambrose Bierce, at the age of seventy.

———

Q. What did the writers Robert Louis Stevenson, Frank Norris, and Jack London have in common?

A. All California writers, none lived beyond the age of forty.

Q. What mural on Stockton Street in San Francisco is half a block long?

A. The Chinatown Mural.

Q. In terms of size, where does the Los Angeles school system rank nationally?

A. Second, behind New York City.

Q. What author was born in San Francisco in 1866 and became known as a muckraker with his articles in the early 1900s?

A. Lincoln Steffens.

Q. What British-born artist moved to Los Angeles in 1963 and drew inspiration from Southern California's pleasure-seeking lifestyle for his contemporary paintings?

A. David Hockney.

Q. What San Francisco-born playwright and producer achieved recognition at the turn of the century for his special stage effects and such plays as *The Girl of the Golden West*?

A. David Belasco.

Q. The first J. Paul Getty Museum opened in what year?

A. 1974.

Q. What Santa Barbara artist made his career painting the California state flower?

A. John Gamble.

Q. The Los Angeles Philharmonic was led by what conductor from 1961 to 1978?

A. Zubin Mehta.

———— ∞ ————

Q. Who was named the state's first poet laureate?

A. Ina Coolbrith.

———— ∞ ————

Q. *They Knew What They Wanted*, which won a Pulitzer Prize in 1924, was written by what California-born playwright?

A. Sidney Howard.

———— ∞ ————

Q. What California author wrote a series of novels about life in her native state from Spanish times to the present?

A. Gertrude Atherton.

———— ∞ ————

Q. With his oil paintings and ceramics, what turn-of-the-century Pasadena artist helped make the rose a symbol of the city?

A. Franz Bischoff.

———— ∞ ————

Q. The dazzling, new Guggenheim Museum in Bilbao, Spain, was designed by what Los Angeles architect?

A. Frank Gehry.

———— ∞ ————

Q. Who created the Southern California detective hero Lew Archer in such novels as *Harper* and *The Drowning Pool*?

A. Ross Macdonald.

SPORTS & LEISURE

Q. What combination athletic contest became an Olympic event at the 1960 Winter Olympics, held in California?

A. The biathlon.

———— ∞∞ ————

Q. Where would one see the original roundhouse and shops of the Sierra Railway?

A. The Railtown 1897 State Historic Park at Jamestown.

———— ∞∞ ————

Q. What Olympic gold medalist contributed greatly to popularizing the swimming "crawl," as well as surfing?

A. Duke Kahanamoku.

———— ∞∞ ————

Q. When UCLA won its sixty-first consecutive basketball game midway through the 1972–73 season, whose record did they break?

A. The University of San Francisco's.

———— ∞∞ ————

Q. The first NFL Pro Bowl was held in what city?

A. Los Angeles.

Q. If not a rattlesnake, to what did the early twentieth-century California ocean fishermen refer by the term "sidewinder"?

A. A simple spool-type fishing reel that attached to the side of the rod.

Q. What NFL star for Detroit and Toronto eventually coached the Los Angeles Kings?

A. Leonard "Red" Kelly.

Q. When did the Summer Olympic Games return to Los Angeles?

A. 1984.

Q. Among California mansions, Death Valley Scotty's Castle was constructed in what architectural style?

A. Spanish-Moorish.

Q. Why are the beautiful beaches of Sinkyone Wilderness State Park nearly deserted?

A. They are almost inaccessible by road.

Q. How many consecutive games did Fernando Valenzuela win in his first Dodger season?

A. Eight, in 1981.

Q. When the USC baseball team won the 1998 College World Series, how many series records were broken or tied?

A. Forty-two records broken—twenty-six records tied.

Q. Who won both the LPGA Rookie of the Year and Player of the Year awards in 1978?

A. Nancy Lopez, born in Torrance.

Q. Hank Aaron hit his 715th homer against what team?

A. The Los Angeles Dodgers, April 8, 1974.

Q. What California site hosted the Winter Olympics in 1960?

A. Squaw Valley.

Q. What area in Southern California offers the greatest concentration of golf courses?

A. A five-square-mile portion of the Palm Springs area, with twenty-two courses.

Q. What was the original name of the "Pea Soup Andersen's" Restaurant in Buellton?

A. Andersen's Electrical Café.

Q. What NFL player tackled opponents for two safeties in one game?

A. Fred Dryer, of the Rams.

Q. Who was the first Oakland A's player to achieve back-to-back 100-RBI seasons?

A. Jose Canseco.

Q. What San Francisco native captured the World Heavyweight Boxing Title?

A. "Gentleman Jim" Corbett, in 1892.

Q. What El Cajon diver set a record that may never be broken, by winning more than one hundred major championships in his career?

A. Greg Louganis.

Q. What amusement park has combined jams, jellies, and roller coasters to attract guests?

A. Knotts Berry Farm, Buena Park.

Q. New York Yankee Joe DiMaggio hailed from what California community?

A. Martinez.

Q. What record did Mario Andretti set when he won the U.S. Grand Prix West at Long Beach in 1977?

A. The first U.S. driver to win a Formula One event held in the United States.

Q. What major league manager "retired" to manage an independent Western League team?

A. Buck Rodgers, the Mission Viejo Vigilantes.

Q. To see huge concrete statues of Amazon warriors, sculpted by a local dentist, one must visit what community?

A. Auburn.

Q. What UCLA and Olympic sprinter ran for one season on her high school boys' track team?

A. Evelyn Ashford.

———— ❧ ————

Q. After playing high school football in LaVerne, who became an All American at West Point?

A. Glenn Davis, who teamed with "Doc" Blanchard to become legendary as a backfield duo known as "Mr. Inside and Mr. Outside."

———— ❧ ————

Q. What one-time Laker held or shared forty-three NBA records, including a one-hundred-point game?

A. Wilt Chamberlain.

———— ❧ ————

Q. Who was the first woman to swim the English Channel ... both ways?

A. Florence Chadwick, a San Diego native.

———— ❧ ————

Q. What state park offers skiing almost directly above Palm Springs?

A. Mount San Jacinto.

———— ❧ ————

Q. What is the name of the four-mile, narrow-gauge railroad in the Sierra National Forest?

A. The Yosemite Mountain Sugar Pine Railroad.

———— ❧ ————

Q. Scoring three touchdowns in a Super Bowl game is a rare achievement, but what player did it twice?

A. Jerry Rice, of the San Francisco 49ers.

Q. Sandy Koufax of the Dodgers and Nolan Ryan, while with the Angels, both threw no-hitters to what catcher?

A. Jeff Torborg.

———— ∞ ————

Q. What L. A. Laker scored an average of at least twenty-five points a game for eleven consecutive NBA seasons?

A. Jerry West.

———— ∞ ————

Q. Measured by the number of animal occupants, where is the world's largest zoo?

A. San Diego.

———— ∞ ————

Q. What Los Angeles land-speed racer set new records by breaking the 400-, 500-, and 600-mile-per-hour barriers?

A. Craig Breedlove.

———— ∞ ————

Q. What is California's only island resort community?

A. Avalon, on Catalina Island.

———— ∞ ————

Q. What native Californian has played for all four major league baseball teams that originated in New York City?

A. Darryl Strawberry (N.Y. Mets, N.Y. Yankees, S.F. Giants, and L. A. Dodgers).

———— ∞ ————

Q. What was the hometown where 1988 Olympic gold medalist Florence Griffith Joyner began running as a child?

A. Los Angeles.

Q. In what city is the world's first surfing museum located?

A. Santa Cruz.

———⚮———

Q. Which NFL team was the first wildcard team to win the Super Bowl?

A. Oakland Raiders.

———⚮———

Q. Who was the Los Angeles native who became the leading U.S. tennis player of the 1950s?

A. "Pancho" Gonzales.

———⚮———

Q. What fifteen-year-old Whittier native won a gold and two silvers at the 1972 Olympics?

A. Shirley Babashoff.

———⚮———

Q. Mary Decker Slaney, who grew up in Huntington Beach, broke what track barrier in 1980?

A. The four-minute mark for the 1,500-meter run.

———⚮———

Q. When he won the 1997 Masters Tournament, how many records did golfer Tiger Woods set?

A. Woods, a Cypress product, set twenty records and tied six.

———⚮———

Q. How were the first animals for the renowned San Diego Zoo acquired in 1916?

A. They remained from the 1915–16 Panama-California Exposition.

Q. What attraction in Klamath is guarded by giant statues of Paul Bunyan and Babe?

A. The Trees of Mystery.

Q. The strip of tourist shops named Santa Claus is located on the coast near what town?

A. Carpenteria.

Q. The generic name attached to linen fishing line by old-time California fishermen was what?

A. Cuttyhunk.

Q. Stanford football star John Elway was drafted by what baseball team two years before being picked in the NFL draft?

A. The New York Yankees, as a second-round choice.

Q. Placentia swimmer Janet Evans set world records in what three swimming events?

A. In the 400-, 800-, and 1,500-meter freestyle.

Q. What is the term for race track winnings carried forth from one race through successive races?

A. "Accumulator." (One 1987 Santa Anita accumulator paid off $1,627,084.)

Q. What California mansion in San Marino features a variety of international gardens?

A. The Huntington Library and Gardens.

Q. Plastic batting helmets were introduced to major league baseball by what team?

A. The Dodgers.

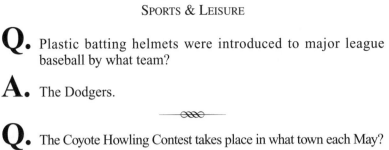

Q. The Coyote Howling Contest takes place in what town each May?

A. Coulterville.

Q. Los Angeles hosted the Special Olympics Summer Games in what year?

A. 1972—there were twenty-five hundred athletes from three countries.

Q. Eddie Feigner and his softball team "the King and His Court" won more than seventy-five hundred softball games against nine-man teams while touring California and the nation, but he often used only how many players?

A. Four: a catcher, shortstop, first baseman; Feigner pitched.

Q. Why was 1958 considered "the year of baseball" for the state of California?

A. The Brooklyn Dodgers moved to Los Angeles, and the New York Giants moved to San Francisco.

Q. What female golfer from San Diego ranks among the all-time LPGA greats, having won more than fifty tournaments?

A. Mickey Wright.

Q. What NBA team was the first to have two players score two thousand points during the same season?

A. The L. A. Lakers (Elgin Baylor and Jerry West, 1964–65).

Q. Disneyland opened in what year?

A. 1955.

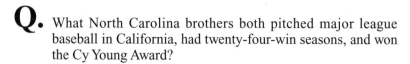

Q. What North Carolina brothers both pitched major league baseball in California, had twenty-four-win seasons, and won the Cy Young Award?

A. Jim and Gaylord Perry.

Q. Oscar De La Hoya of Los Angeles has won boxing championships in how many different weight classes?

A. Four, although as of 1998 he was shooting for six.

Q. Chris Evert lost in the 1974 Los Angeles Virginia Slims to whom?

A. Evonne Goolagong.

Q. The Los Angeles Dodgers won their first World Series in what year?

A. 1960.

Q. A golfer on the "Dad" Miller golf course must be in what city?

A. Anaheim.

Q. A feature event at the National Date Festival in Indio is what?

A. Camel races.

Q. To eat with fingers (compulsory) while being entertained by prancing horses and jousting knights, one must be where in Southern California?

A. Medieval Times, at Buena Park.

Q. Because of the local cartoonist who built it, Santa Rosa's ice arena is known as the "home ice" of whom?

A. Snoopy (drawn by cartoonist Charles Schulz).

Q. How many paved and lighted airports are found in California?

A. Approximately seven hundred.

Q. Ted Williams, the last baseball player to hit at least .400 (as of 1998), was a native of what city?

A. San Diego.

Q. What January event is sponsored in the nearby mountains by Palm Springs?

A. Sled dog races.

Q. In the 1935 NCAA track and field championships in Berkeley, Jesse Owens won how many individual titles?

A. Four.

Q. The NHL Lady Byng trophy for "high standard of playing" and "sportsmanship" went to whom in both 1996 and 1997?

A. Paul Kariya, of the Anaheim Mighty Ducks.

Q. Ranked by storage capacity, which California winery is nearly six times larger than its nearest competitor?

A. E & J Gallo.

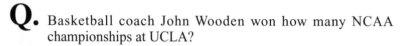

Q. Basketball coach John Wooden won how many NCAA championships at UCLA?

A. Ten.

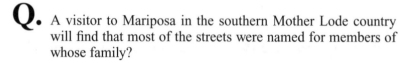

Q. A visitor to Mariposa in the southern Mother Lode country will find that most of the streets were named for members of whose family?

A. Col. John C. Frémont's.

Q. What cowboy star became principal owner of the California Angels?

A. Gene Autry.

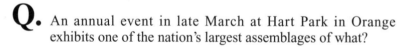

Q. An annual event in late March at Hart Park in Orange exhibits one of the nation's largest assemblages of what?

A. Model A Fords.

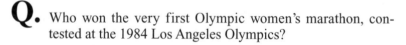

Q. Who won the very first Olympic women's marathon, contested at the 1984 Los Angeles Olympics?

A. Joan Benoit Samuelson.

Q. How many people attended the first Rose Bowl Parade on January 1, 1890?

A. Only two thousand.

Q. When did Lew Alcindor change his name to Kareem Abdul-Jabbar?

A. 1971.

Q. There are how many sporting-goods stores in the state?

A. Nearly seven thousand.

Q. Former Angels pitcher Nolan Ryan broke whose major league record for career strikeouts?

A. Walter Johnson.

Q. Listening to the one-hundred-bell carillon in the California Tower, one must be where?

A. San Diego's Balboa Park, where the two-hundred-foot tower emits chimes every quarter hour.

Q. The classy Pond in Anaheim is home to what hockey team?

A. The Mighty Ducks.

Q. What is the main tourist attraction in Salinas?

A. The Steinbeck House and Library.

Q. In addition to the five islands that make up the Channel Islands National Park, two others in the group are controlled by whom?

A. The U.S. Navy.

Q. Jackie Robinson competed in baseball, football, and track at what university?

A. UCLA.

Q. In conjunction with its Pageant of the Masters, what town hosts a series of art festivals?

A. Laguna Beach.

Q. Notre Dame's Knute Rockne coached in what bowl game, the only one of his career?

A. The Rose Bowl.

Q. What museum displays the stuffed carcass of a well-known horse?

A. The Roy Rogers Museum, at Victorville (the horse is Trigger).

Q. How did the Los Angeles Lakers get their name?

A. They originated in Minneapolis, the "City of Lakes," in the late 1940s.

Q. The Sonoma-Cutrer Vineyards in Windsor hosted what world championships in 1994?

A. The World Croquet Championships.

Q. Pasadena's Rose Bowl was built in what year?

A. 1922.

Q. Sandy Koufax led the National League in earned-run average for how many consecutive years?

A. Five.

⸺∞⸺

Q. What player grabbed the most rebounds in a single NCAA Final Four game?

A. Bill Russell (twenty-five in the 1955 title game against LaSalle).

⸺∞⸺

Q. What hotel is famous for its cave rooms?

A. The Madonna Inn, in San Luis Obispo.

⸺∞⸺

Q. The oldest racetrack west of the Mississippi is located where?

A. Pleasanton.

⸺∞⸺

Q. Maureen Connolly, a dominant tennis player from 1944 to 1954, had what nickname?

A. Little Mo.

⸺∞⸺

Q. What Pac-10 basketball player recorded the first conference triple double?

A. Kevin Johnson of UC Berkeley, in 1987 (twenty-two points, twelve assists, and ten rebounds).

⸺∞⸺

Q. What San Diego native went on to become an internationally renowned yacht racer as winner of the America's Cup?

A. Dennis Conner.

Q. Which Dodgers pitcher won the Rookie of the Year, MVP, and Cy Young awards during his career?

A. Don Newcombe.

Q. What is the oldest working thoroughbred farm west of the Mississippi?

A. Stonepine, built in 1930 in the Carmel Valley.

Q. What race car driver was the first to sweep all three major California events?

A. David Pearson, in 1975.

Q. What three-sport performer pitched 139 no-hitters, 41 perfect games, and struck out Ted Williams and Hank Aaron along the way?

A. Joan Joyce, basketball All-American, professional softball pitcher, and LPGA golfer.

Q. What is the name of the choice surfing location near Pillar Point in San Mateo County?

A. Maverick's.

Q. UCLA players have won the NCAA Final Four Outstanding Player Award how many times?

A. Nine.

Q. What city hosted the 1993 National Yo-Yo Championship?

A. Chico.

Q. The 2,400-mile hiking trail that follows the mountain summit ridgelines from Canada to Mexico is called what?

A. The Pacific Crest Trail.

Q. California's oldest courthouse, built in Mariposa in 1854, sports what unique addition?

A. A tower clock, brought around Cape Horn in 1866.

Q. Who won the men's and women's figure skating singles events at Squaw Valley in 1960?

A. David Jenkins and Carol Heiss, both of the United States.

Q. What is one of the country's largest ski areas with one of the longest seasons?

A. Mammoth Mountain.

Q. Once welcoming only unwilling visitors, Alcatraz now hosts how many voluntary guests per year?

A. About 750,000.

Q. What major league team was once called the Robins?

A. The Dodgers.

Q. The only redwood-covered bridge in the United States is in what California town?

A. Felton.

Q. The remarkable Eddie Murray, an L. A. native, was one of how many brothers to play professional baseball?

A. Five.

—⊗⊗⊗—

Q. How does the Pac-10 stack up against the Big Ten in Rose Bowl victories for the years 1948 to 1997?

A. Pac-10, twenty-six wins; Big Ten, twenty-four.

—⊗⊗⊗—

Q. What is the mascot of the University of California at Santa Cruz?

A. The banana slug.

—⊗⊗⊗—

Q. Among NBA coaches, who reached the 900-career-win mark most quickly?

A. Former L. A. Lakers coach Pat Riley.

—⊗⊗⊗—

Q. Former Dodgers pitcher Don Sutton pitched at least two hundred innings in each of how many seasons?

A. Twenty.

—⊗⊗⊗—

Q. Long regarded as one of the nation's premier airshows, what event closed forever in 1997?

A. The El Toro Airshow, terminated because of the impending Marine Air Station closure.

—⊗⊗⊗—

Q. What Huntington Beach horse trainer combined in 1998 with the horse Real Quiet to win the Preakness and Kentucky Derby, and then lose the Belmont Stakes by inches?

A. Bob Baffert.

Q. When he called it "the most beautiful meeting of land and sea on earth," Robert Louis Stevenson referred to what?

A. What is now the Point Lobos State Reserve, at the southern end of the Monterey Peninsula.

Q. Where is California's only beachside amusement park?

A. The Beach Boardwalk, in Santa Cruz.

Q. What is San Francisco's hands-on museum that deals with the human senses called?

A. The Exploratorium.

Q. First in so much, the Golden State ranks where in the number of bowling facilities?

A. Fifth among the states, with 340.

Q. What Long Beach native became the first woman athlete to earn more than $100,000 in one year?

A. Tennis player Billie Jean King, in 1971.

Q. Where is the Rosicrucian Egyptian Museum?

A. San Jose.

Q. What Irvine resident broke the English Channel swim record in 1994?

A. Chad Hundeby, in seven hours and seventeen minutes.

Q. What old stagecoach route in the Napa Valley is now one of the most popular bicycling roads in the state?

A. The Silverado Trail.

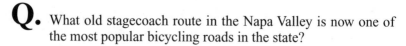

Q. After a brilliant major league career, Mel Ott briefly managed what California team?

A. Oakland, of the Pacific Coast League.

Q. Who received a special award, created for him by the International Volleyball Federation, naming him the "world's best volleyball player"?

A. Karch Kiraly, in 1986.

Q. The "Fearsome Foursome" comprised an awesome defensive line for what team?

A. The Los Angeles Rams (Lamar Lundy, Merlin Olsen, Rosey Grier, and Roger Brown).

Q. What mansion is a landmark on Catalina Island?

A. The Wrigley mansion, built by the one-time owners of the island.

Q. What fish ranks as the most popular prey for California anglers?

A. Freshwater trout, surprisingly, are more popular than ocean fish.

Q. While leading USC to four straight NCAA championships, what swimmer captured four gold medals and one silver medal at the 1976 Olympics?

A. John Naber.

Q. After becoming the first race-car driver to break the mile-a-minute barrier, who finished his career as a Hollywood consultant?

A. Barney Oldfield.

Q. What was the first California team to win the NCAA basketball championship?

A. Stanford, over Dartmouth in 1942.

Q. Which hotel boasts the most expensive accommodation in the state?

A. The Fairmont Hotel, in San Francisco, offers its eight-room penthouse at $6,000 per night.

Q. Of the four Rose Bowl games he coached, how many did John Robinson win?

A. All four.

Q. Deaf from birth, what Anaheim teenager excelled at platform diving and then went on to success in water skiing, land-speed driving, water-speed racing, and Hollywood stunt work?

A. Kitty O'Neil.

Q. When did a heavyweight boxer last win the title in a fight staged in California?

A. April 27, 1968, when Jimmy Ellis defeated Jerry Quarry in Oakland.

Q. What national monument contains more than three hundred tube caves, some larger than subway tunnels?

A. Lava Beds.

Q. A Santa Monica native, who broke the sixty-foot shotput barrier in 1954?

A. Parry O'Brien.

———

Q. What pitcher won 111 games, three Cy Young awards, and an MVP award, pitched four no-hitters, and played on teams that won three pennants and two world championships—all from 1962 through 1966?

A. Dodger Sandy Koufax, despite missing much of one season with arm trouble.

———

Q. Which resort boasts the most hot tubs in California?

A. Sycamore Mineral Springs, near San Luis Obispo.

———

Q. Which of the tourist attraction Gold Rush ghost towns watched its population shrink from ten thousand to zero?

A. Bodie, in the Mammoth Lakes area.

———

Q. Which former Los Angeles Laker entered the Basketball Hall of Fame on May 15, 1995?

A. Kareem Abdul-Jabbar.

———

Q. The full name of the great one-time 49er quarterback, Y. A. Tittle, was what?

A. Yelberton Abraham Tittle.

———

Q. What national monument features campgrounds at elevations ranging from minus 198 feet to plus 8,133 feet?

A. Death Valley.

Q. What school did UCLA defeat in basketball fifty-two consecutive times?

A. UC Berkeley.

———

Q. What UCLA tennis player (1962–66) became a professional star and eventually launched a fundraising campaign to combat AIDS?

A. Arthur Ashe.

———

Q. What Oakland Raider center, labeled by many as "too small," entered the NFL Hall of Fame in 1980?

A. Jim Otto.

———

Q. What thoroughbred racehorse won the 1940 Santa Anita Handicap and dominated the sport from 1935 to 1940?

A. Seabiscuit.

———

Q. In the first NFL draft (1936), what college had the most players drafted?

A. Stanford.

———

Q. At which California resort can guests participate in half-day cattle drives?

A. The Alisal Guest Ranch and Resort, near Solvang.

———

Q. The Sisson Fish Hatchery, once the world's largest and now a museum, is found where?

A. Mount Shasta.

Q. Construction on the 160-room Winchester Mystery House in San Jose began in 1880 and continued for how many years?

A. Thirty-eight, until the death of Sarah Winchester.

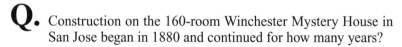

Q. Many of the skis crafted by Scandinavians in 1850s California were made of what?

A. Barrel staves.

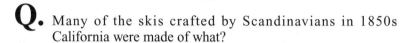

Q. An outstanding defensive lineman, what Los Angeles Ram was elected to Phi Beta Kappa and held two degrees in economics?

A. Merlin Olsen, who has also distinguished himself in broadcasting and acting.

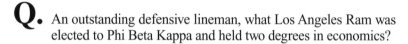

Q. Which left-handed pitcher who pitched a number of years with the Dodgers won more than two hundred career games, yet never had a twenty-win season?

A. Jerry Reuss.

Q. Where will one find the largest single-span, double-reversible aerial tramway in the world?

A. The Palm Springs Aerial Tramway up the side of Mount San Jacinto, the steepest mountain in North America.

Q. What NBA coach with California ties was drafted in the eleventh round by the Dallas Cowboys?

A. Pat Riley, coming out of the University of Kentucky, in 1967.

Q. When it first became part of the Winter Olympics at Squaw Valley in 1960, what was the biathlon called?

A. The Military Ski Patrol.

Q. What American skier, the first to win two Olympic gold medals, finished her career by carrying the torch down Papoose Peak at Squaw Valley in 1960?

A. Andrea Mead Lawrence.

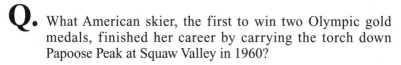

Q. What museum poses guests for photos next to a life-sized likeness of a popular musician?

A. The Lawrence Welk Museum, in Escondido.

Q. What native of Centerville became an international tennis star, dubbed "Little Poker Face"?

A. Helen Moody.

Q. Already a national diving champion, who became a doctor and then an Olympic champion?

A. Sammy Lee, a native of Fresno.

Q. What Long Beach fixture—encompassing restaurants, shops, and a hotel—has seen Europe over a thousand times?

A. The *Queen Mary*.

Q. What native Californian won the only gold medal awarded to an American at the 1968 Winter Olympics?

A. Peggy Fleming, in women's figure skating.

Q. What dam backs up four rivers to form the largest manmade lake in the state, a prime water recreation area?

A. Shasta (Lake Shasta).

Q. Tommy Lasorda managed the Dodgers to how many World Series titles?

A. Two, 1981 and 1988.

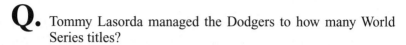

Q. Who won Olympic gold medals in both springboard and platform in 1952 and in 1956?

A. Pat McCormick, of Lakewood.

Q. What California location was once the spring training site for the Chicago Cubs?

A. Catalina Island, owned exclusively at the time by William Wrigley Jr.

Q. As of 1998, Shaquille O'Neal was the last center to win what NBA award?

A. Rookie of the Year.

Q. What Death Valley tourism site was named for an historical activity that occurred elsewhere?

A. Twenty-Mule Team Canyon.

Q. What is the oldest working lighthouse on the Pacific Coast?

A. The Battery Point Lighthouse, built in 1856, on an island off the Del Norte County coast.

Q. Which Southern California hotel, nicknamed the "Pink Palace," is famous for its Polo Lounge?

A. The Beverly Hills Hotel.

Q. Chosen the best player in the World Volleyball Championships in Bourgas, Bulgaria, who went on to win the television *Superstars* competition and become a professional coach?

A. Mary Jo Peppler.

———

Q. What San Diego Padre was drafted by two teams in the same city on the same day?

A. Tony Gwynn, in 1981 by the Padres baseball team and the San Diego Clippers basketball team.

———

Q. At what California inn can one sleep in a fifties Cadillac convertible, a Roman chariot, or a gypsy wagon?

A. The Victorian Mansion, in Los Alamos.

———

Q. Wayne Gretzky, who spent part of his career playing for the L. A. Kings, won the NHL MVP award how many consecutive times?

A. Eight.

———

Q. What was the first major league baseball team that Casey Stengel managed?

A. The (Brooklyn) Dodgers.

———

Q. Losing eighteen straight road games (1977–1979) was the ignominy achieved by which NFL team?

A. The San Francisco 49ers.

———

Q. Although it sounds like a boxing term, the *knucklebuster* actually referred to what?

A. An early Pacific Ocean fishing reel, with a simple leather flap pressed by the thumb as the drag.

Q. What city, known for its Victorian homes, is built on the northernmost natural harbor?

A. Eureka.

Q. In summer, many of the ski slopes of the Mammoth Mountain area are used for what?

A. Mountain biking.

Q. What is Disneyland's three-deck sternwheeler steamboat named?

A. The *Mark Twain*.

Q. California was the first state to host at least how many major league baseball All-Star Games?

A. Nine.

Q. Situated among thousands of Spanish and Indian names, the city of Menlo Park traces its name to what country?

A. Ireland (the name was adapted from Menlough).

Q. Earvin "Magic" Johnson played on three championship teams at three levels in a span of how many years?

A. Four (1977–80): state high school (Michigan), NCAA (Michigan State), and NBA (Lakers).

Q. At what museum can you learn what it's like to be trapped in tar?

A. La Brea Tar Pits Museum, in Los Angeles.

Q. Although invented by Polynesians, surfing was introduced to Redondo Beach by whom?

A. George Freeth, 1907.

———⊗⊗⊗———

Q. What water skiing champion won the Olympic decathlon before turning to stunt planes and race cars?

A. Bruce Jenner.

———⊗⊗⊗———

Q. Where is the largest Chinese quarter outside the Orient?

A. San Francisco's Chinatown, a twenty-four-block area, bordered by Grant Avenue and Stockton Street.

———⊗⊗⊗———

Q. When he called it "the grandest of all the special temples of Nature I was ever permitted to enter," John Muir was referring to what?

A. The area that has become Yosemite National Park.

———⊗⊗⊗———

Q. The largest interpretive railroad museum in the country is found where?

A. Old Sacramento—a large museum, Central Pacific Depot, and steam train rides.

———⊗⊗⊗———

Q. What communities form the southern and northern gates of the Seventeen-Mile Drive?

A. Carmel and Pacific Grove, respectively.

———⊗⊗⊗———

Q. A visitor to the Wells Fargo Express Building in Sonora may choose to take what two kinds of rides?

A. Horseback or stagecoach.

Q. What area, called "America's Sahara," is a favorite of fossil and rock hunters, as well as drivers of dune buggies?

A. The Imperial Sand Dunes, east of El Centro, were also used in filming *Lawrence of Arabia*.

Q. Which desert ghost town, restored by Walter Knott, offers visitors thirty miles of tunnels?

A. Calico, north of Barstow.

Q. In addition to 350 days of sunshine, what resort area offers approximately 200 golf tournaments annually?

A. The Coachella Valley.

Q. From urban, sunny Los Angeles, one has to travel how far to enjoy snow skiing?

A. About forty miles, to the popular Mount Baldy ski area.

Q. The name Old Sacramento refers to what?

A. A twenty-eight-acre national historic landmark near the state capitol.

Q. The recently remodeled villa in Malibu, known for its Greek and Roman collections, is what?

A. The Getty Museum.

Q. What one-time Angels pitcher tossed seven no-hitters in his major league career?

A. Nolan Ryan.

Q. Prior to Tommy Lasorda, who was the only other manager of the Dodgers?

A. Walter Alston.

———∞∞———

Q. What Dodger made three errors in one World Series game?

A. Outfielder Willie Davis dropped two fly balls and made an errant throw during Game Two of the 1966 World Series against the Baltimore Orioles.

———∞∞———

Q. What nonkicker led the National Football League in scoring in 1987?

A. San Francisco 49ers wide receiver Jerry Rice, with 138 points.

———∞∞———

Q. What NFL team "owns" *Monday Night Football?*

A. The Oakland Raiders, which entered the 1998 season with a 30–11–1 record on Monday nights.

———∞∞———

Q. Where was the first Super Bowl played?

A. Los Angeles Coliseum, in 1967 (Green Bay beat Kansas City, 35–10).

———∞∞———

Q. In the ten-year span of 1964 to 1973, how many NCAA national titles did coach John Wooden's UCLA teams win?

A. Nine (the Bruins missed in 1966).

SCIENCE AND NATURE

C H A P T E R   S I X

Q. What are the tallest living things in the world?

A. California redwoods.

———— ∞ ————

Q. Campers and hikers might encounter which kind of bear in the wild regions of California?

A. The black bear.

———— ∞ ————

Q. La Jolla is the home of what famous institute of oceanography?

A. Scripps.

———— ∞ ————

Q. What Chinese method of pain relief treatment first found U.S. acceptance in California?

A. Acupuncture.

———— ∞ ————

Q. Forests cover about what percentage of the total land area of California?

A. 40 percent.

Q. "Spanish pear" and "green gold" are among the nicknames for what Southern California fruit?

A. Avocado.

Q. What local species of insect lives in pools of crude oil, feeding on other insects that become trapped in the oil?

A. The California petroleum fly.

Q. Mount Shasta Ski Bowl was the site of what U.S. meteorological record set in February 1959?

A. The most snow in a single storm, 189 inches, February 13–19, 1959.

Q. How many states host a larger variety of plants than California?

A. None. No other state even comes close.

Q. Of the species of trout found in the southern high Sierra Nevada, which is native to the area?

A. The golden trout.

Q. What phenomenon involving ocean currents in the eastern Pacific occurs every five to ten years and affects weather over much of the planet?

A. *El Niño.*

Q. What is California's state flower?

A. The golden poppy.

Q. Where is the highest cluster of rock art in North America to be found?

A. The Coso Range Petroglyphs, created thousands of years ago, in the northern Mojave Desert.

Q. What female American astronaut went on to become the director of the California Space Institute at U.C. San Diego?

A. Sally K. Ride.

Q. The year 1964 marked the end of the payment of bounties for what wild animal?

A. The mountain lion.

Q. What well-known volcano in the Cascades has two cones?

A. Mount Shasta.

Q. About a dozen workers died during the construction of what Depression Era structure?

A. The Golden Gate Bridge, completed in 1937.

Q. Raging hillside brushfires set the stage for what other natural disaster?

A. Mudslides caused by winter rains.

Q. People across America came to enjoy fresh California fruits and vegetables in the 1880s because of what new development?

A. Refrigerated railroad boxcars.

Q. The largest solar power plant in the world is located east of what city?

A. Barstow.

———— ∞ ————

Q. In 1955, U.C. Berkeley physicists synthesized what element?

A. Mendelevium, atomic number 101, named after the Russian chemist Mendeleyev, who devised the basis for the periodic table.

———— ∞ ————

Q. The eastern Sierra Nevada ranks as an important world source of what mineral?

A. Tungsten.

———— ∞ ————

Q. What portion of the early grasslands that covered one-fourth of the state remains?

A. Approximately 1 percent.

———— ∞ ————

Q. Hollywood filmmaking broke into the realm of "big business" with the development of what technology?

A. Talkies—movies with sound.

———— ∞ ————

Q. Which California observatory is also equipped with seismographic equipment?

A. The Lick Observatory, at U.C. Santa Cruz.

———— ∞ ————

Q. The wholesale plant industry was changed by what California innovation of the 1930s?

A. Growing plants in cans.

Q. Although trout are found in many streams and lakes, what is the only high-country lake that contained trout prior to the Gold Rush?

A. Tahoe.

Q. Known for their width, giant sequoias can have trunks that are how thick?

A. Up to thirty-six feet in diameter.

Q. How fast do the migrating gray whales swim?

A. Typically seven miles per hour.

Q. Tests at the University of California determined what two colors best for car safety?

A. Dark blue for daylight and fog—yellow for night.

Q. The shape of its leaves brought what plant the nickname "holly oak"?

A. The California live oak.

Q. While most states have only one climatic zone (few more than four), California has how many?

A. Twenty-four.

Q. Where was the Internet first conceived?

A. At UCLA, about 1970.

Q. The largest of California's carnivorous plants is known as what?

A. The California pitcher plant, or cobra lily.

Q. How many kinds of elk inhabit the state?

A. Three: Roosevelt, Tule, and Rocky Mountain.

Q. Although environmentalist John Muir's name is attached to many natural attractions, his home, part of John Muir National Historic Site, is located in which town?

A. In Martinez, on Alhambra Avenue.

Q. California Institute of Technology, often called Cal Tech, was founded in 1891 by whom?

A. Amos Gager Throop.

Q. What is the largest flying bird in North America?

A. The California condor.

Q. The incredibly light substance, silica aerogels, weighing only five ounces per cubic foot, was produced in 1990 at what California laboratory?

A. Lawrence Livermore.

Q. After raiding the nests of other birds, which bird found in California replaces the eggs with its own?

A. Cowbird.

Q. What was unique about the geothermal energy plant established in Sonoma County in 1922?

A. It was the first in the United States (there are now many such plants in the area).

———— ∞ ————

Q. What is Gilbert's skink?

A. A lizard, found in the chaparral regions of California.

———— ∞ ————

Q. Some Californians know that the full name of *El Niño* is what?

A. *El Niño de Navidad* (because it typically commences before Christmas in December).

———— ∞ ————

Q. Who was the U.S. physicist, a professor and director of the Berkeley Radiation Laboratory, who invented the cyclotron particle accelerator?

A. Ernest Lawrence.

———— ∞ ————

Q. What biologist won the Darwin medal, the Copley medal, the Nobel Prize, and led Cal Tech to become a prominent genetic research center?

A. Dr. Thomas Hunt Morgan.

———— ∞ ————

Q. Where does the state's highest annual precipitation occur?

A. In the Siskiyou Mountains of northwest California, an average of about 140 inches.

———— ∞ ————

Q. In the terms of plate tectonics, a region where one plate slides past another is called what?

A. Conservative margin. An example is the well-known San Andreas fault.

Q. The state's lowest recorded temperature, registered at Boca in 1937, was what?

A. Minus forty-five degrees Fahrenheit.

Q. Reaching from New York to San Francisco, what was the nation's first transcontinental highway?

A. The Lincoln Highway, officially designated U.S. Route 30 in 1925, two years after its completion.

Q. What unusual wetland habitat exists in the arid high desert of the Owens Valley?

A. Fish Slough. (Because it is spring-fed, it survives on less than six inches of annual rainfall.)

Q. In 1939, two young Stanford grads joined forces in a Palo Alto garage to form what company?

A. Hewlett Packard.

Q. When did the practice of stocking trout in California lakes begin?

A. In 1819, when golden trout were moved from a drying creek channel to Cottonwood Lakes.

Q. Where would one find the Griffith Planetarium, and what would one expect to see there?

A. In Los Angeles, a realistic display of celestial movements projected on screens.

Q. Willard Frank Libby, a former UCLA professor of chemistry, developed what archaeological process?

A. The carbon-14 dating technique.

Q. Early California Indians used the lateral fiber of what plant for ropes, fishnets, hats, and blankets?

A. The lateral fiber of yucca leaves.

Q. What two aircraft rolled off the Douglas Aircraft assembly lines approximately twenty years apart and became leaders in the air transport industry?

A. The DC-3, the early workhorse; and the DC-8, the first jet transport by Douglas.

Q. The annual open house hosted by California State Polytechnic University at San Luis Obispo is called what?

A. Poly Royal.

Q. What actress and animal-rights activist runs a refuge for large cats in Southern California?

A. Tippi Hedren.

Q. Which observatory was opened in 1948 and was regarded as the world's best for the next decade?

A. Mount Palomar.

Q. While California is known to many as "earthquake country," the state suffers more frequently from what two enemies?

A. Fires and mudslides.

Q. What sets the Tehachapi Mountains apart from most California ranges?

A. Referred to as a transverse range, they run east and west.

Q. The largest winter gathering of bald eagles in the forty-eight contiguous states takes place where?

A. The Tule Lake National Wildlife Refuge, in the Klamath Basin.

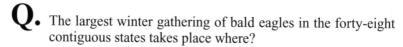

Q. When other cities are parched, Palm Springs gets along nicely, drawing water from what source?

A. The desert oasis draws all the water it needs from an underground aquifer ... for now.

Q. What is the insect that takes four generations to migrate from Canada through California to Mexico and back?

A. The monarch butterfly.

Q. What professor of chemistry served at four California schools and took unpopular stands against nuclear weapons and the Vietnam War?

A. Dr. Linus Carl Pauling.

Q. What California rodent harvests and plants seeds and shares its burrows with other animals?

A. The giant kangaroo rat hosts the blunt-nosed leopard lizard and the San Joaquin antelope squirrel.

Q. The two Keck telescopes, the world's largest optical telescopes, are jointly owned by the California Institute of Technology and the University of California, and are located where?

A. Mauna Kea, Hawaii.

Q. What is California's state tree?

A. The California redwood.

Q. Of what magnitude on the Richter scale was the San Francisco earthquake of April 18, 1906?

A. It was measured at 8.3.

Q. In 1935, Pan American Airways inaugurated what new service?

A. Their China Clipper "flying boat" service across the Pacific.

Q. What is the only species of turtle native to California?

A. The western pond.

Q. For every thousand-foot gain in elevation from the floor of Death Valley, the temperature drops how much?

A. A little more than four degrees Fahrenheit.

Q. People who grow and harvest date trees are called what?

A. Palmeros.

Q. What seems to be the principal result of the many powerful prehistoric California earthquakes?

A. Violent plate movements ruptured the surface and created most of the mountain ranges.

Q. Who was the California professor of physics who directed the development of the first atomic bombs (1943–1945) and later stood opposed to the hydrogen bomb?

A. J. Robert Oppenheimer.

Q. Blue Canyon holds what U.S. meteorological record?

A. The highest average annual snowfall, 241 inches.

Q. What three names did it outlive before becoming known as California Institute of Technology?

A. Throop University, Throop Polytechnic Institute, and Throop College of Technology.

Q. What is the world's tallest tree?

A. The Howard Libbey Redwood—361 feet tall.

Q. Where are California's natural hot springs located?

A. While Calistoga is perhaps the best known, hot springs are widely scattered about the state.

Q. How many lakes are there in California?

A. About eight thousand.

Q. What comet, photographed by astronomers at Mount Wilson Observatory in 1913, became the first observed throughout its orbit?

A. Encke's comet.

Q. Who flew the *Voyager* on the first unrefueled, nonstop round-the-world flight, beginning and ending at Edwards Air Force Base in 1986?

A. Dick Rutan and Jeana Yeager.

Q. What is the only California lighthouse in which one can stay overnight?

A. East Brother Light Station, on an island between San Francisco and San Pablo Bays.

———∞———

Q. Fed only by freshwater rivers and streams, what inland body of water is extremely salty?

A. The Salton Sea.

———∞———

Q. The rain shadow that has caused the Great Basin Desert is caused by what?

A. The mighty stone barrier of the Cascades and the Sierra Nevada.

———∞———

Q. California generates how much of its electricity from non-polluting waterpower?

A. About 20 percent.

———∞———

Q. When nature-loving Californians speak of the "Elfin Forest," they refer to what?

A. The miles and miles of chaparral, a low-profile ecosystem.

———∞———

Q. What world-famous observatory was closed from 1985 to 1993 for lack of funding?

A. Mount Wilson closed when the Carnegie Institution dropped its support.

———∞———

Q. The San Andreas fault is part of what belt of faults and volcanoes that encircles the Pacific?

A. Ring of Fire.

Q. The first coast-to-coast airborne shipment of what agricultural product took place in 1944?

A. The first cut flowers were shipped from California.

Q. Why are there so many eucalyptus trees in Rancho Santa Fe?

A. The railroad imported and cultivated them, believing (incorrectly) they would provide good railroad ties.

Q. Scientists have retrieved fossils that are more than forty thousand years old from what tar pits?

A. La Brea.

Q. By 1920, the population of the Tule elk herd had reached an all-time low of how many?

A. Twenty-eight. But through careful management, they have made a steady comeback.

Q. The loud, screechy rattle often heard along California streams can be traced to what bird?

A. The belted kingfisher.

Q. California rivers that must remain undammed and be allowed to follow their natural course are classified as what?

A. "Wild and scenic."

Q. Judge James Logan, a California botanist, crossed wild blackberries with red raspberries to produce what?

A. The loganberry.

Q. What is the name of the NASA center for deep space probes, and where is it located?

A. The Jet Propulsion Laboratory, at Pasadena.

———— ∞∞∞ ————

Q. Although California's dams produce electricity with minimal air pollution, they have what negative effect?

A. They seriously impact the ecosystems downstream.

———— ∞∞∞ ————

Q. The Grand Canyon (5,500 feet) is not the deepest canyon in the United States: what is?

A. Kings Canyon (8,200 feet).

———— ∞∞∞ ————

Q. What town holds the nation's record for the longest period without rain?

A. Bagdad, in the Mojave Desert (767 days).

———— ∞∞∞ ————

Q. How many plants are native to California?

A. More than five thousand.

———— ∞∞∞ ————

Q. The John Muir Trail, paralleling the summit of a portion of the Sierra Nevada, is how long?

A. About 210 miles.

———— ∞∞∞ ————

Q. What fish lays its eggs on land?

A. The California grunion.

Q. What four-inch-long creature lives only in the Sacramento and San Joaquin Rivers?

A. The delta smelt, a tiny blue fish that is struggling for survival.

Q. People descend on which community every March 19 to watch the swallows return?

A. San Juan Capistrano.

Q. In this century, man has tampered with how much of the state's coastal wetlands?

A. More than 60 percent of the coastal wetlands has been drained, dredged, or filled.

Q. Of the ten largest national parks in the lower forty-eight states, which three are in California?

A. Death Valley National Monument, Yosemite National Park, and Joshua Tree National Monument.

Q. Often called the "high desert," what is the average elevation of the Mojave Desert?

A. Approximately thirty-six hundred feet.

Q. Edwards AFB hosted the return of what vehicle after its maiden flight?

A. The space shuttle *Columbia*, 1981.

Q. The famous telescope launched into outer space was named for whom?

A. Edwin Powell Hubble, who specialized at Mount Wilson in galactic and extragalactic systems.

Q. Why was Mike Kasperak's surgery (Stanford Medical Center, 1968) significant?

A. He was the first adult heart-transplant recipient in the United States.

Q. The largest known prime number, determined in 1989 by California researchers after a year of computation, has how many digits?

A. 65,087 digits.

Q. What is California's state bird?

A. The California valley quail.

Q. What high desert lake is known for its brine shrimp and flies?

A. Mono, in the eastern Sierra Nevada.

Q. The "Climbing Cecile Brunner," acclaimed in Riverside in the late nineteenth century, refers to what?

A. A new rose hybrid.

Q. What marine mammal, seen along the California coast, often carries a rock to dislodge its prey and crack the prey's shell?

A. The sea otter, which can be seen floating on its back, carrying its weapon on its belly.

Q. Hydroponics, a growing California industry involving the cultivation of plants without soil, mixes water and solutions of what?

A. Mineral salts.

Q. Which direction does the California current flow along the coastline?

A. Southward.

Q. In the volcanic Cascades of Northern California, what are the two major peaks?

A. Mount Shasta (14,162 feet) and Mount Lassen (10,457 feet).

Q. During which months do Californians see the most migrating gray whales?

A. December and January for southbound whales; March and April for northbound whales.

Q. Who was the U.S. astronomer, a leader in studies of the sun, who established three important observatories, among them Mount Wilson and Mount Palomar?

A. George Ellery Hale.

Q. The monarch butterfly feeds on what, thereby protecting itself against predators?

A. Poisonous milkweed.

Q. How long is the longest span of the Golden Gate suspension bridge?

A. Forty-two hundred feet.

Q. The Tasmanian *Eucalyptus globulus* and the Sydney *Eucalyptus saligna* trees, now common to California, are often known by what name?

A. Blue gum trees.

Q. Which California valley contained the largest lake west of the Mississippi in the late 1800s?

A. The San Joaquin.

———∞———

Q. For what invention was Donald Arthur Glaser, a University of California professor, awarded the Nobel Prize for physics in 1960?

A. The bubble chamber used to detect and study nuclear particles.

———∞———

Q. How was Yosemite Valley formed?

A. By a glacier during the Ice Age.

———∞———

Q. What is California's most visible fault?

A. Some might say smog, but it's the San Andreas fault, portions of which are readily visible.

———∞———

Q. What is the state animal of California?

A. The grizzly bear, although now extinct in California.

———∞———

Q. While the millions of cars in Southern California create much of the Los Angeles smog, what natural topographical feature contributes to the situation?

A. The mountains to the north and east keep the smog from moving on.

———∞———

Q. The theory of the quark was established by what Cal Tech physicist?

A. Murray Gell-Mann, a 1969 Nobel Prize winner.

Q. The Pioneer Series of planetary probes traces to which NASA installation?

A. Ames Research Center, at Mountain View.

Q. What is California's deepest lake?

A. Tahoe reaches 1,650 feet in depth.

Q. The famous Hoover Dam is surpassed in height by which California dam?

A. Oroville rises to 754 feet, compared to the Hoover at 726 feet.

Q. Who was the Cal Tech scientist who shared the 1958 Nobel Prize for his work in biochemistry based upon the one gene-one enzyme hypothesis?

A. George Wells Beadle.

Q. How have California harbor seals adapted to deep diving?

A. They exhale to avoid the bends, yet they can dive to one thousand feet and remain submerged for twenty minutes.

Q. What famous physician and microbiologist developed a vaccine against polio and eventually lent his name to the Institute for Biological Studies, U.C. San Diego?

A. Dr. Jonas Edward Salk.

Q. Among the many varieties of palm trees in Southern California, which is native to the state?

A. The California palm, of course.

Q. In 1949, which synthesized, radioactive, metallic element of the actinide series was attributed to the Glenn Seaborg team of physicists?

A. Berkelium.

———⦿———

Q. What area along the San Andreas fault has been a focal point for geophysical research?

A. The Cienega Valley, where ongoing plate slippage has been measurable.

———⦿———

Q. Seafarers navigating the long California coastline are impacted by what unusual feature?

A. The few protected harbors along the 840-mile shoreline.

———⦿———

Q. Where among the states does California rank in terms of threatened species?

A. First among the continental United States, with more than six hundred kinds of plants listed as threatened.

———⦿———

Q. The collection of tall basalt pillars formed southwest of Mammoth Mountain is called what?

A. Devil's Postpile National Monument.

———⦿———

Q. What is the largest of the Sierra squirrels?

A. The yellow-bellied marmot, a relative of the midwestern and eastern woodchuck.

———⦿———

Q. For what type of agriculture is the Lompoc area best known?

A. Flowers for seed purposes.

Q. The sheer rock walls of Half Dome are found where?

A. Yosemite Valley, in the Sierra Nevada.

Q. Quasars (quasi-stellar radio sources) were first identified in 1963 by astronomers at which observatory?

A. Palomar.

Q. Because of the northwest movement of the Pacific tectonic plate, what city theoretically will reach the latitude of San Francisco in approximately ten million years?

A. Los Angeles.

Q. Who shared the 1951 Nobel Prize for Chemistry with Glenn Seaborg for producing plutonium?

A. Edwin M. McMillan, 1940.

Q. What is the largest desert in the United States?

A. Southern California's Mojave Desert, with an area of fifteen thousand square miles.

Q. Much of the California coastline was created by what geological process?

A. Prehistoric earthquakes lifted the coast range out of the sea.

Q. Where can a variety of tiny sea creatures be easily observed on any day?

A. In the coastal tide pools at low tide.

Q. In yet another effort to reduce air pollution while generating electricity, California hosts large fields of what?

A. Electricity-generating windmills.

Q. How far does the San Andreas fault extend through the state of California?

A. Over seven hundred miles, from northwest to southeast.

Q. Unlike most California mountains, the Cascade Range was formed by what?

A. Volcanic action.

Q. The acorns of which oak tree are considered to be the most palatable?

A. The acorns of the blue oak supported California Native-American tribes, as well as birds and mammals.

Q. In 1906 Paul Ecke discovered and nurtured what plant that would become a holiday tradition?

A. The poinsettia.

Q. Strangely, in addition to anchovies, squid, and shrimps, sea lions are known to ingest what?

A. Stones, as much as sixty-five pounds in some cases.

Q. Among the causes of declining populations of various California birds, a common denominator is what?

A. Chlorinated hydrocarbons, such as DDT and DDE, that cause thin eggshells.

Q. How many peaks of the Sierra Nevada reach beyond fourteen thousand feet?

A. Twelve.

Q. Calcium deposits form unusual moonlike landscapes in the waters of what lake?

A. Mono.

Q. Why did so many animals get caught in the Rancho La Brea tar seeps?

A. The tar was covered by veneerlike pools of water that disguised the danger.

Q. Volcanic Mount Lassen erupted occasionally between 1914 and 1917, but when did Mount Shasta last erupt?

A. In 1786.

Q. While not native to California, what creature became the official state marine mammal in 1976?

A. The gray whale.

Q. The first Los Angeles trolleys drew their power from what source?

A. They were horse-drawn.

Q. The tanoak tree was so named because of what?

A. It once provided a large proportion of the tannin used to tan leather.

Q. Which U.S. waterfall has the greatest total drop?

A. Yosemite Falls, Yosemite National Park. Three sections combine for a drop of 2,425 feet.

Q. What is unique about Methuselah, the bristlecone pine tree that lives in the White Mountains?

A. At an estimated age of forty-seven hundred years, it is the oldest known living thing in the world.

Q. Scientists generally agree that global warming of three to five degrees Fahrenheit would expand the oceans, bringing about what effect in California?

A. A rise of over twenty feet in sea level and accompanying coastal flooding.

Q. The Sierra Nevada, the state's primary geological feature, is composed mostly of what rock?

A. Granite.

Q. Who occupied Alcatraz before the establishment of the penal institution?

A. One of the largest west coast colonies of pelicans—*alcatraz* means pelican in Spanish.

Q. What is the world's longest linac (linear accelerator), the device used to bring charged particles to high speeds and energy?

A. The Stanford Linear Collider is two miles long.

Q. What UC Berkeley chemist won the 1961 Nobel Prize for chemistry?

A. Melvin Calvin, for his work in photosynthesis.

Q. How long ago, according to human bone finds, was man known to exist in California?

A. At least forty-eight thousand years.

Q. How does the precipitation compare between the north and south slopes of the transverse mountain ranges?

A. At seventeen inches per year, the north slopes get about half as much as the south slopes.

Q. Dried grapes (raisins) hold most of their nutritional value, but only what percentage of their original weight?

A. Twenty-five percent.

Q. What did California's first endangered-species law, written in 1874, protect?

A. The sea otter.

Q. The thickness of the tectonic plates, such as the one beneath North America, is estimated in feet, yards, or miles?

A. Miles—some are more than thirty miles thick.

Q. Which side of the Sierra Nevada is considered to be the "dry side"?

A. East.

Q. When Southern Californians refer to the Saddleback, they speak of what?

A. The saddle-shaped contour of Santiago and Modjeska Peaks.

Q. Among California deserts, what is unusual about the precipitation pattern of the Great Basin?

A. Most of its precipitation falls in the winter as snow.

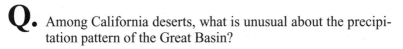

Q. What bird of the cuckoo family runs up to fifteen miles per hour, can fly but seldom does, and is more than a match for a small- to medium-sized rattlesnake?

A. The roadrunner.

Q. What developments enabled Southern California to become the nation's most populous area?

A. The California, Los Angeles, and Colorado aqueducts.

Q. What annual migration follows the west coastline for six thousand miles each way?

A. The gray whales migrate from the Bering Sea to Baja and back again.

Q. The locations of the numerous hot springs in the state generally relate to what?

A. The locations of faults.

Q. Since young Joshua trees are favorite targets of rodents, how do any survive?

A. By germinating and then living under the protective cover of other shrubs for several years.

Q. What sag-pond lake in Southern California is filled with purchased water?

A. Elsinore, in Riverside County, with purchased water from the Colorado River.

Q. In the autumn, Southern California's forests and brush-covered hillsides become fire-prone tinderboxes because of what?

A. Hot Santa Ana winds blowing in from the deserts, coupled with the effects of the dry season.

Q. What is the form of knowledge representation that depends upon context, and therefore cannot be precisely defined?

A. Fuzzy logic, the label chosen by computer scientist Lofti Zadeh at UC Berkeley in 1965.

Q. The alpine zone of California's mountains refers to what?

A. The area above the treeline.

Q. Where was the first refuge created for waterfowl in the United States?

A. The Klamath Wildlife Refuge on the California-Oregon border, created in 1908.

Q. Who is credited with designing the first waterbed?

A. Charles Hall, a San Francisco State University student.

Q. The California laurel tree *(Umbellularia californica)* carries what name in Oregon?

A. The Oregon Myrtle, famous for carvings made of its wood.

Q. How often is the Golden Gate Bridge repainted?

A. It is a perpetual project; upon reaching one end, the painters start over at the other.

Q. Environmentalist John Muir persuaded which presidents to set aside the first forest reservations?

A. Grover Cleveland and Theodore Roosevelt.

Q. How much remains of the eight million acres of natural habitat of the San Joaquin Valley?

A. Approximately 4 percent.

Q. Of the tourist attraction aquariums about the world, which has the largest single-pane window?

A. The Monterey Bay Aquarium.

Q. What is the typical difference in depth between California high and low tides?

A. Ten to fifteen feet.

Q. The scale by which seismographs measure earthquakes was developed in 1935 by whom?

A. Geologist Charles Richter, of Cal Tech.

Q. What seemingly flat valley actually slopes upward three hundred feet from north to south?

A. The San Joaquin Valley.

Q. What is the name of the largest sequoia?

A. General Sherman. It stands 273 feet tall and is over 36 feet thick at the base.

Q. What scientific developments enabled early European seafarers to find and explore California?

A. The compass, along with improved ship building, cartography, and celestial navigation.

Q. The completion of what massive project sent electricity to Los Angeles in 1936?

A. Boulder Dam (later called Hoover Dam).

Q. The efforts of Philo Farnsworth in a 1920s San Francisco laboratory led to what?

A. Television.

Q. How do scientists believe Lake Tahoe was created?

A. Prehistoric glaciers carved deep canyons, then later melted, filling them with water.

Q. A process invented by former Cal Tech student Chester F. Carlson led ultimately to the formation of what corporation?

A. His electrostatic copy process led to the Xerox Corporation.

Q. If the subspecies *Sequoia gigantea* is found in the Sierra Nevada, what relative is found in the coastal mountains?

A. *Sequoia sempervirens.*

Q. Whose experiments led to sixty varieties of plums?

A. Luther Burbank's.